MASTERING ADOBE INDESIGN 2024 GUIDE FOR BEGINNERS

CORELAR SHARNANDEZ

INTRODUCTION

Welcome to "Mastering Adobe InDesign 2024: A Guide for Beginners." This comprehensive guide is designed to help you navigate the powerful world of Adobe InDesign 2024, an industry-leading software for page design and layout. Whether you're a novice just starting or someone with some experience looking to deepen your knowledge, this book provides the insights and practical knowledge needed to master InDesign.

Adobe InDesign has long been a cornerstone in the publishing and design industries. Its versatility allows users to create everything from simple flyers and brochures to complex magazines, books, and interactive digital publications. InDesign 2024 continues this tradition, introducing a host of new features and enhancements aimed at streamlining the design process and expanding creative possibilities.

The Evolution of Adobe InDesign

Adobe InDesign has evolved significantly since its inception, continually adapting to the changing needs of designers and publishers. The 2024 version marks another milestone in this evolution, offering tools and features that reflect the latest trends in digital and print design.

One of the standout features of InDesign 2024 is its improved user interface, designed to provide a more intuitive and efficient workflow. This includes enhancements to workspace customization, allowing users to tailor the interface to their specific needs and preferences. Additionally, the integration of UXP plugins opens new doors for creativity and functionality, enabling designers to extend InDesign's capabilities with custom tools and scripts.

Key Feature Updates

InDesign 2024 brings several key updates that enhance both functionality and user experience. The Auto Style feature, for instance, automates the application of styles to text and objects, saving time and ensuring consistency across documents. Hide Spreads is another valuable addition, allowing users to streamline their workspace by hiding unnecessary spreads during the design process.

The new Filename Suffix feature simplifies file management, automatically adding suffixes to filenames to keep track of different versions and edits.

Meanwhile, the Publish Online function has been improved, making it easier to share interactive documents on the web. Integrating Google Analytics with Publish Online provides valuable insights into how your digital publications are being accessed and used.

Enhancing User Experience

InDesign 2024 places a strong emphasis on user experience and precision. The integration of HarfBuzz, a text shaping engine, ensures more accurate text rendering and layout, particularly for complex scripts and languages. This improvement is crucial for designers working on multilingual projects or those requiring intricate typographic details.

The introduction of UXP plugins represents a significant advancement in extending InDesign's capabilities. These plugins offer a new level of customization and functionality, empowering users to create tailored tools that enhance their workflow. Whether you need a specific design feature or an automation script, UXP plugins provide the flexibility to adapt InDesign to your unique requirements.

Setting Up for Success

Getting started with InDesign 2024 involves setting up your workspace to suit your workflow. This guide covers everything from customizing the home screen to configuring the tools and panels you use most frequently. By setting up a personalized workspace, you can streamline your design process and work more efficiently.

InDesign's workspace customization options include the ability to create and save custom workspaces, dock and undock panels, and scale the user interface to your preferences. These features ensure that you can work in a way that feels natural and intuitive, minimizing distractions and maximizing productivity.

Creating and Managing Documents

Creating documents in InDesign 2024 is a seamless process, thanks to an array of templates and presets designed to get you started quickly. Whether you're designing a simple flyer or a complex magazine, InDesign provides the tools you need to create professional-quality documents with ease.

The New Document dialog offers a comprehensive overview of available templates and presets, allowing you to choose the best starting point for your project. From there, you can customize your document settings to match your specific needs, ensuring that your designs meet the highest standards of quality and precision.

Mastering Text and Typography

Text and typography are at the heart of any InDesign project. InDesign 2024 offers robust tools for adding, formatting, and managing text, allowing you to create visually appealing and readable layouts. The software's advanced typographic settings, including nested styles and OpenType features, provide the flexibility to achieve the desired look and feel for your text.

Working with text frames, paragraph and character styles, and nested styles allows you to maintain consistency and efficiency in your design process. Whether you're importing text from external sources or creating it directly within InDesign, the software's powerful text tools ensure that your content is always presented in the best possible way.

Integrating Images and Graphics

InDesign 2024 simplifies the process of working with images and graphics, offering tools for inserting, resizing, and formatting visual elements within your documents. The Place command, along with advanced image fitting options, ensures that your images are always displayed correctly and with the highest quality.

Managing images through the Links panel allows you to keep track of all the visual elements in your document, making it easy to update or replace images as needed. Additionally, InDesign's support for vector graphics and integration with other Adobe Creative Cloud apps ensures that you can create and manipulate graphics with precision and ease.

Color Management and Effects

Effective color management is crucial for producing high-quality designs, whether for print or digital output. InDesign 2024 offers a range of tools for applying color to text and objects, using swatches for consistency, and adding special effects to enhance your designs.

The software's color management features ensure that your colors are always accurate and consistent, from the initial design stages to the final output. Whether you're working with spot colors, color libraries, or custom color settings, InDesign provides the tools you need to achieve the perfect look for your project.

Interactive and Digital Publishing

InDesign 2024 expands its capabilities beyond print, offering powerful tools for creating interactive and digital publications. Whether you're adding hyperlinks, buttons, or forms, InDesign makes it easy to create engaging and interactive documents that can be viewed on a variety of devices.

The software's Publish Online function allows you to share your interactive documents with a global audience, while integration with Google Analytics provides insights into how your content is being accessed and used. This combination of tools ensures that your digital publications are not only visually appealing but also effective in reaching and engaging your audience.

Collaboration and Version Control

Collaboration is a key aspect of modern design workflows, and InDesign 2024 offers robust tools for working with others. Integration with Adobe InCopy allows for seamless collaborative editing, enabling multiple users to work on the same document simultaneously.

Version control features help you keep track of changes and manage different versions of your documents, ensuring that your team is always working with the most up-to-date content. These collaboration tools are essential for teams working on large and complex projects, providing the structure and control needed to manage multiple contributors effectively.

Prepress and Printing

Preparing your documents for print involves a series of steps to ensure that everything is set up correctly and meets the required standards. InDesign 2024 offers comprehensive prepress and printing tools, including preflighting, PDF export, and support for various PDF/X standards.

These tools help you verify that your documents are print-ready, identifying any potential issues before they become problems. By using InDesign's prepress features, you can ensure that your printed materials meet the highest standards of quality and accuracy.

Automation and Efficiency

Efficiency is a key factor in any design process, and InDesign 2024 offers several tools to help you work faster and more effectively. Automation and scripting features allow you to automate repetitive tasks, freeing up more time for creative work.

By writing and executing custom scripts, you can tailor InDesign to your specific needs and streamline your workflow. Whether you're automating complex processes or creating custom shortcuts, InDesign's scripting capabilities provide the flexibility to enhance your productivity and efficiency.

Troubleshooting and Optimization

Even with the best tools, challenges can arise during the design process. InDesign 2024 includes features to help you troubleshoot common issues and optimize performance. From resolving text overflow and image quality concerns to managing layers and recovering from crashes, this guide provides practical solutions to keep your projects on track.

Optimizing InDesign's performance, especially for large documents, involves configuring settings and preferences to minimize resource usage and maximize efficiency. By following best practices for performance optimization, you can ensure that InDesign runs smoothly, even with complex and resource-intensive projects.

Advanced Typography and Customization

InDesign 2024 offers advanced typography techniques, including OpenType features and the ability to implement ligatures, swashes, and alternate characters. These tools allow you to create sophisticated typographic designs that stand out and capture attention.

Customization options, including the creation and management of plugins and extensions, provide additional ways to tailor InDesign to your specific needs. By leveraging these advanced features, you can push the boundaries of your design work and create truly unique and compelling layouts.

Conclusion

"Mastering Adobe InDesign 2024: A Guide for Beginners" is your comprehensive resource for learning and mastering this powerful design tool. From setting up your workspace and creating basic documents to exploring advanced typography and interactive features, this guide covers all aspects of InDesign 2024.

Whether you're designing for print or digital, working alone or as part of a team, this book provides the knowledge and tools you need to succeed. By following the practical tips and techniques outlined in this guide, you'll be well on your way to becoming a proficient and confident InDesign user, capable of creating stunning and professional-quality designs.

CONTENTS

CHAPTER 1: INTRODUCING TO INDESIGN

I. WHAT IS ADOBE INDESIGN?

Overview of Adobe InDesign

Adobe InDesign is a powerful desktop publishing and typesetting software application developed by Adobe Systems. Since its initial release in 1999, InDesign has become the industry standard for creating a wide variety of print and digital media. It is extensively used by graphic designers, publishers, and marketing professionals for designing and laying out everything from brochures, magazines, newspapers, and books to posters, flyers, and digital publications like eBooks and interactive PDFs.

InDesign's versatility and integration with other Adobe Creative Cloud applications, such as Photoshop and Illustrator, make it an essential tool for any creative professional. It allows users to create complex, multi-page documents with rich graphics, advanced typography, and precise control over layouts and styles. Whether you're designing a simple one-page flyer or an elaborate magazine spread, InDesign provides the tools and functionalities needed to bring your vision to life.

Key Features and Capabilities

Adobe InDesign boasts a wide array of features and capabilities that cater to both beginners and seasoned professionals. Here are some of its key features:

1. **Intuitive Layout and Design Tools**

    - **Pages and Master Pages**: InDesign's Pages panel lets you manage and organize pages efficiently. Master pages enable you to create consistent layouts by applying templates to multiple pages, saving time and ensuring uniformity.

- **Guides and Grids**: These tools help in aligning and positioning elements precisely, providing a structured layout and maintaining consistency throughout the document.

- **Frames and Shapes**: InDesign uses frames to hold text and images. You can create and manipulate frames and shapes, enabling flexible and creative design options.

2. **Advanced Typography**

- **Character and Paragraph Styles**: Define and apply consistent text formatting across your document with character and paragraph styles. This feature is particularly useful for lengthy documents, ensuring typographic consistency.

- **OpenType Support**: InDesign supports OpenType fonts, offering advanced typographic features like ligatures, stylistic sets, and alternate characters, enhancing the text's visual appeal.

- **Text Flow and Linking**: Manage large amounts of text with ease by flowing text across multiple pages or linking text frames. This ensures that your text is displayed correctly, even as you make changes to the layout.

3. **Comprehensive Graphic Design Tools**

- **Image Handling**: Place, resize, and crop images seamlessly. InDesign maintains the original image quality, and you can link to external files to keep your project size manageable.

- **Integration with Adobe Creative Cloud**: InDesign integrates seamlessly with other Adobe applications like Photoshop and Illustrator, allowing you to import and edit graphics directly within your layout.

- **Effects and Transparency**: Apply effects such as drop shadows, glows, and transparency settings to text and objects, adding depth and visual interest to your designs.

4. **Interactive and Digital Publishing**

- **Interactive PDFs**: Create interactive documents with hyperlinks, buttons, forms, and multimedia elements like audio and video. This capability is essential for creating engaging digital content.

- **ePub and HTML Export**: Export your documents as ePub or HTML for eBooks and web content, ensuring your designs are accessible on various digital platforms and devices.

- **Digital Magazines and Apps**: With Adobe Digital Publishing Solution (DPS), you can design and publish interactive digital magazines and apps, expanding your reach to mobile audiences.

5. **Prepress and Production**

   - **Preflight and Packaging**: InDesign's preflight feature checks your document for potential issues before printing, such as missing fonts or low-resolution images. The packaging feature gathers all files, including fonts and graphics, into a single folder, making it easy to share with printers or collaborators.

   - **Print Specifications**: Define print specifications like bleed, slug, and crop marks, ensuring your document is print-ready and meets professional standards.

   - **Color Management**: Utilize color swatches, Pantone libraries, and ICC profiles to manage colors accurately, ensuring consistent output across different devices and media.

6. **Collaboration and Cloud Integration**

   - **Adobe Creative Cloud Libraries**: Store and access assets like logos, images, and color swatches in Creative Cloud Libraries, enabling easy collaboration and consistency across projects.

   - **Share for Review**: Share your InDesign documents with clients or team members for review and feedback. The comments are integrated directly into the InDesign interface, streamlining the revision process.

   - **Version History**: Keep track of changes and revert to previous versions if needed, ensuring you never lose important work.

Benefits of Using Adobe InDesign

1. **Efficiency and Productivity**: InDesign's user-friendly interface and powerful tools streamline the design process, allowing you to create professional-quality layouts quickly and efficiently. Features like master pages, styles, and templates save time and reduce repetitive tasks.

2. **Creative Freedom**: With InDesign, you have the freedom to experiment with layouts, typography, and graphics. The software's extensive design tools and integration with Adobe Creative Cloud open up endless creative possibilities.

3. **Professional Output**: InDesign ensures your documents meet professional standards, whether for print or digital media. The preflight and packaging features help catch potential issues early, and the color management tools ensure accurate color reproduction.

4. **Versatility**: InDesign is versatile enough to handle a wide range of projects, from simple flyers to complex, multi-page publications. Its digital publishing capabilities also make it a valuable tool for creating interactive and online content.

5. **Industry Standard**: As the industry standard for desktop publishing, proficiency in InDesign is a valuable skill for graphic designers, publishers, and marketing professionals. It's widely used in various industries, making it a crucial tool for anyone looking to pursue a career in design or publishing.

Conclusion

Adobe InDesign is an essential tool for anyone involved in graphic design, publishing, or marketing. Its comprehensive set of features and capabilities enables users to create professional-quality layouts and designs efficiently. Whether you're a beginner or an experienced designer, mastering InDesign can significantly enhance your productivity and creative output, making it a valuable addition to your skill set.

II. DEVELOPMENT HISTORY OF ADOBE INDESIGN

Early Beginnings and Evolution

Adobe InDesign's origins can be traced back to the late 1990s when Adobe Systems sought to create a professional desktop publishing (DTP) tool that would surpass the limitations of existing software. Prior to InDesign's development, Adobe's main DTP product was Adobe PageMaker, a program that, while revolutionary at its inception, began to lag behind in terms of features and performance compared to competitors like QuarkXPress.

The journey began in 1999 when Adobe introduced Adobe InDesign 1.0. This launch marked a significant shift in the DTP landscape, as InDesign was built from the ground up using modern code, making it more stable and versatile than its predecessors. Adobe aimed to address the needs of professional designers and publishers who required a robust tool capable of handling complex layouts, advanced typography, and high-quality print production.

Major Milestones and Updates

Since its initial release, Adobe InDesign has undergone numerous updates and enhancements, each bringing new features and improvements that solidified its position as the industry standard for desktop publishing. Here are some of the major milestones in InDesign's development history:

1. **Adobe InDesign 1.0 (1999)**

   - **Introduction**: The first version of InDesign introduced a user-friendly interface, support for OpenType fonts, and advanced typographic controls. It also featured robust integration with Adobe Photoshop and Illustrator.

   - **Competitive Edge**: Unlike its competitors, InDesign offered support for Unicode and advanced transparency effects, setting a new standard for design software.

2. **Adobe InDesign 2.0 (2002)**

   - **Key Features**: This version introduced long-awaited features such as multiple undo, text on a path, and advanced table creation tools. It also improved integration with other Adobe products.

- **Innovations**: InDesign 2.0 was the first major application from Adobe to support the newly introduced Portable Document Format (PDF) version 1.4, enhancing its prepress capabilities.

3. **Adobe InDesign CS (2003)**

- **Creative Suite Integration**: The introduction of Adobe Creative Suite (CS) brought InDesign into a tightly integrated suite of Adobe applications, including Photoshop, Illustrator, and Acrobat.

- **New Features**: InDesign CS introduced features like nested styles, the ability to create and manage object libraries, and enhanced text wrap options.

4. **Adobe InDesign CS2 (2005)**

- **Enhanced Productivity**: This version focused on productivity enhancements, such as the ability to create object styles, anchored objects, and improved image handling.

- **Adobe Bridge**: InDesign CS2 integrated with Adobe Bridge, a file management tool that streamlined the workflow across Adobe applications.

5. **Adobe InDesign CS3 (2007)**

- **Universal Binary**: InDesign CS3 was optimized for Intel-based Macs, making it faster and more efficient.

- **New Tools**: It introduced new tools like the Multi-File Place feature, which allowed designers to import multiple files simultaneously, and the ability to create interactive PDFs with hyperlinks and buttons.

6. **Adobe InDesign CS4 (2008)**

- **Enhanced Usability**: This version focused on usability improvements, including the addition of a new live preflight feature, conditional text, and the ability to create and manage multiple page sizes within a single document.

- **Interactivity**: InDesign CS4 made it easier to create interactive documents and presentations, supporting export to SWF and other interactive formats.

7. **Adobe InDesign CS5 (2010)**

- **Digital Publishing**: With the rise of digital media, InDesign CS5 introduced new tools for digital publishing, including the Folio Builder panel for creating interactive digital magazines.

- **New Features**: This version also added features like object states, improved animation tools, and the ability to create multiple versions of a layout for different devices and orientations.

8. **Adobe InDesign CS6 (2012)**

    - **Liquid Layouts**: This feature allowed designers to create flexible layouts that adapt to different screen sizes and orientations.

    - **Alternate Layouts**: InDesign CS6 introduced the ability to create alternate layouts within the same document, making it easier to design for multiple devices and platforms.

9. **Adobe InDesign CC (2013-Present)**

    - **Creative Cloud Integration**: The transition to Adobe Creative Cloud marked a significant shift, as InDesign became part of a subscription-based service. This allowed for more frequent updates and seamless integration with other Adobe apps and services.

    - **Continuous Improvements**: Over the years, Creative Cloud versions of InDesign have introduced numerous enhancements, including improved performance, enhanced typography features, better EPUB export options, and more robust collaboration tools.

Adobe InDesign 2024: What's New?

Adobe InDesign 2024 continues the tradition of innovation and improvement, bringing a host of new features and enhancements designed to meet the evolving needs of designers and publishers. Here are some of the standout features in this latest version:

1. **AI-Powered Design Tools**

    - **Adobe Sensei Integration**: InDesign 2024 leverages Adobe Sensei, Adobe's artificial intelligence and machine learning platform, to provide intelligent design suggestions and automation. This includes auto-layout adjustments, color palette recommendations, and content-aware fit for images.

2. **Enhanced Collaboration**

    - **Real-Time Co-Editing**: Multiple users can now edit the same document simultaneously, with real-time updates and conflict resolution. This feature is a game-changer for teams working on complex projects.

    - **Improved Review and Feedback**: The Share for Review feature has been enhanced with more robust commenting and annotation tools, making it easier to gather and implement feedback from stakeholders.

3. **Advanced Typography and Layout Features**

    - **Variable Fonts**: InDesign 2024 introduces full support for variable fonts, allowing designers to fine-tune weight, width, and other attributes for more precise typographic control.

- **Grid and Layout Enhancements**: New grid and layout tools provide more flexibility in designing complex, multi-column layouts. This includes improved support for custom grid systems and enhanced snapping options.

4. **Digital Publishing and Interactive Content**

   - **Enhanced EPUB Export**: The EPUB export workflow has been streamlined, with improved support for reflowable and fixed-layout EPUBs. New options for adding interactivity and multimedia elements enhance the digital reading experience.

   - **Interactive PDFs**: Creating interactive PDFs is now easier, with new tools for adding animations, video, and interactive forms directly within InDesign.

5. **Performance and Stability Improvements**

   - **Faster Rendering**: InDesign 2024 includes performance enhancements that make working with large, complex documents smoother and more efficient.

   - **Stability**: Adobe has focused on improving the stability of InDesign, addressing common crash scenarios, and optimizing memory usage.

6. **Accessibility and Compliance**

   - **Enhanced Accessibility Tools**: New features make it easier to create accessible documents that comply with accessibility standards, including improved tagging, reading order management, and enhanced support for screen readers.

Conclusion

Adobe InDesign has come a long way since its debut in 1999, evolving from a promising newcomer to the industry standard for desktop publishing. With each new version, Adobe has introduced features and enhancements that address the changing needs of designers and publishers, ensuring that InDesign remains a powerful and versatile tool for creating both print and digital content. The 2024 version continues this tradition of innovation, offering new AI-powered tools, enhanced collaboration features, and advanced typography options that further cement its status as an essential tool for creative professionals.

III. HOW TO SMART LEARNING INDESIGN

Learning Strategies and Resources

Adobe InDesign is a powerful tool for creating professional-quality layouts and designs, but mastering it can seem daunting for beginners. To make your learning journey efficient and effective, it's essential to adopt smart learning strategies and leverage a variety of resources.

1. Set Clear Goals:

- Define what you want to achieve with InDesign. Whether you're looking to create brochures, magazines, eBooks, or presentations, having clear goals will help you stay focused and motivated.

2. Break Down Learning into Manageable Chunks:

- Instead of trying to learn everything at once, break down the software into key components such as basic tools, text formatting, image handling, and advanced features. Tackle each component one at a time.

3. Practice Regularly:

- Consistent practice is crucial. Apply what you learn by working on small projects or exercises that reinforce new skills. This hands-on approach helps solidify your understanding and build confidence.

4. Use a Blended Learning Approach:

- Combine different types of learning resources—videos, articles, books, and practical exercises—to cater to various learning styles and enhance retention.

5. Seek Feedback:

- Share your work with peers, mentors, or online communities to get constructive feedback. This will help you identify areas for improvement and learn from others' experiences.

6. Stay Updated:

- Adobe frequently updates InDesign with new features and enhancements. Follow Adobe's official blog, attend webinars, and join forums to stay informed about the latest updates and best practices.

Online Tutorials and Courses

The internet is a treasure trove of tutorials and courses that cater to different skill levels, from beginners to advanced users. Here are some popular platforms and resources to consider:

1. Adobe Learn:

- **Adobe Learn** (https://helpx.adobe.com/indesign/tutorials.html) offers a wide range of free tutorials that cover the basics of InDesign as well as advanced techniques. These tutorials are created by Adobe experts and provide step-by-step instructions.

2. LinkedIn Learning:

- Formerly known as Lynda.com, LinkedIn Learning provides comprehensive courses on InDesign. These courses range from beginner to advanced levels and are taught by industry professionals. The platform also offers quizzes and project files to enhance learning.

3. Udemy:

- Udemy hosts numerous InDesign courses that cover various aspects of the software. These courses are often on sale and include lifetime access, allowing you to learn at your own pace.

4. Skillshare:

- Skillshare offers a variety of InDesign classes, many of which are project-based. This hands-on approach helps learners apply their skills in practical scenarios.

5. YouTube:

- YouTube is a great resource for free InDesign tutorials. Channels like **Envato Tuts+, Terry White, and Satori Graphics** provide high-quality content that can help you master different features of InDesign.

6. Coursera:

- Coursera offers courses from top universities and institutions. While not exclusively focused on InDesign, some courses cover graphic design principles and software usage, including InDesign.

Books and Guides

Books and guides are valuable resources for structured learning and deep dives into specific topics. Here are some recommended books for learning InDesign:

1. "Adobe InDesign Classroom in a Book (2024 release)" by Kelly Kordes Anton and Tina DeJarld:

- This official training series from Adobe is a comprehensive guide that covers all aspects of InDesign. It includes real-world projects and step-by-step lessons, making it an excellent resource for beginners and advanced users alike.

2. "InDesign for Beginners: A Step-by-Step Guide to Mastering InDesign" by Scott Casterson:

- This book is perfect for beginners looking for a straightforward introduction to InDesign. It covers the basics of the software and provides practical examples to help you get started.

3. "Adobe InDesign CC: A Complete Course and Compendium of Features" by Stephen Laskevitch:

- This book is a detailed guide that covers both the foundational skills and advanced techniques in InDesign. It includes a wealth of illustrations and practical exercises to enhance learning.

4. "Adobe InDesign CC Classroom in a Book (2021 release)" by Kelly Kordes Anton and Tina DeJarld:

- Another edition of the official Adobe training series, this book provides thorough coverage of InDesign CC's features and workflows, making it a valuable reference for all users.

5. "Real World Adobe InDesign CC" by Olav Martin Kvern, David Blatner, and Bob Bringhurst:

- This book is aimed at professional users and covers advanced topics such as automation, scripting, and complex layouts. It's a great resource for those looking to deepen their expertise.

Community Support and Forums

Engaging with the InDesign community can provide additional support, inspiration, and opportunities for collaboration. Here are some ways to connect with other InDesign users:

1. Adobe Support Community:

- The Adobe Support Community (https://community.adobe.com/) is a forum where you can ask questions, share tips, and connect with other InDesign users. Adobe experts and community members regularly contribute to discussions, providing valuable insights.

2. Reddit:

- Subreddits like **r/indesign** and **r/graphic_design** are great places to ask questions, share your work, and get feedback from a global community of designers.

3. Facebook Groups:

- Facebook groups such as **Adobe InDesign User Group** and **InDesign Secrets** offer a platform for users to share tips, ask for help, and stay updated on the latest news and tutorials.

4. LinkedIn Groups:

- Professional groups on LinkedIn, like **Adobe InDesign Enthusiasts** and **Graphic Design Professionals**, provide opportunities to network with industry peers, share knowledge, and learn about job opportunities.

5. Meetup:

- Meetup.com hosts various design and InDesign-specific groups where you can attend workshops, webinars, and networking events in your local area or online.

6. Online Design Communities:

- Websites like **Behance** and **Dribbble** allow you to showcase your work, get inspired by other designers, and connect with potential collaborators or clients.

Conclusion

Learning Adobe InDesign efficiently requires a combination of clear goals, regular practice, and the use of diverse learning resources. Online tutorials and courses provide structured and flexible learning opportunities, while books and guides offer in-depth knowledge and reference material. Engaging with the InDesign community through forums and social media groups can provide valuable support, feedback, and inspiration. By leveraging these strategies and resources, you can master InDesign and use it to create stunning, professional-quality designs.

IV. SUBSCRIPTION PURCHASE AND PRICE

Adobe InDesign, part of Adobe Creative Cloud, offers various subscription plans tailored to different users' needs, including individual creatives, businesses, and educational institutions. Understanding the subscription options, pricing, and available benefits can help you make an informed decision that best suits your requirements.

Adobe InDesign Subscription Plans

1. Individual Plans:

- **Single App Plan:** This plan is ideal for users who only need Adobe InDesign. It includes access to the latest features and updates, 100GB of cloud storage, Adobe Portfolio, Adobe Fonts, and Adobe Spark. Users also get access to Adobe's extensive library of tutorials and the ability to sync settings across multiple devices.

- **Creative Cloud All Apps Plan:** For those who require more than just InDesign, this plan offers access to the entire suite of Adobe Creative Cloud applications, including Photoshop, Illustrator, After Effects, Premiere Pro, and more. It also includes 100GB of cloud storage and other Creative Cloud services.

2. Business Plans:

- **Single App for Teams:** Similar to the individual single app plan but tailored for business use. It includes centralized administration, license management, and advanced technical support.

- **All Apps for Teams:** This plan provides access to all Creative Cloud applications and is designed for businesses that need multiple Adobe tools. It includes additional features like 24/7 tech support, unlimited job postings on Adobe Talent, and team collaboration tools.

3. Educational Plans:

- **Student and Teacher Plans:** Adobe offers significant discounts for students and teachers on both the Single App and All Apps plans. These plans provide the same features as the standard individual plans but at a reduced price, making it more accessible for educational purposes.

- **Schools and Universities:** These plans are designed for institutions that need to provide Adobe software to large groups of students and faculty. They include device-based licenses and volume licensing options, along with administrative tools for deployment and management.

Pricing Options and Packages

Adobe's pricing options vary depending on the subscription plan and region. Here's an overview of typical pricing for different plans:

1. Individual Plans:

- **Single App Plan:** Approximately $20.99 per month for InDesign alone. Prices may vary based on promotional offers or regional pricing.

- **Creative Cloud All Apps Plan:** Approximately $54.99 per month, offering access to the full suite of Adobe Creative Cloud applications.

2. Business Plans:

- **Single App for Teams:** Approximately $33.99 per month per license. This plan includes additional business-oriented features like enhanced support and administrative tools.

- **All Apps for Teams:** Approximately $79.99 per month per license, providing access to all Creative Cloud applications and business-specific benefits.

3. Educational Plans:

- **Student and Teacher Single App Plan:** Around $19.99 per month, with the All Apps plan available for about $29.99 per month. These discounted rates are available to verified students and educators.

- **Schools and Universities:** Pricing for educational institutions varies based on the number of licenses and specific requirements. Institutions can contact Adobe for custom quotes and volume discounts.

Free Trial and Student Discounts

Free Trial:

- Adobe offers a 7-day free trial for InDesign and other Creative Cloud applications. This trial provides full access to all features and capabilities, allowing users to explore the software and determine if it meets their needs before committing to a subscription. The trial is available for both individual and business users.

Student Discounts:

- Adobe provides substantial discounts for students and educators to make its software more accessible for learning and teaching. To qualify for student pricing, users must verify their enrollment or employment status at an accredited institution. The verification process typically involves providing a school email address or proof of enrollment.

Promotions and Offers:

- Adobe frequently runs promotional offers, such as discounts on annual plans or bundled packages. Keeping an eye on Adobe's official website and subscribing to their newsletter can help you stay informed about any upcoming deals.

Subscription Benefits

Subscribing to Adobe InDesign as part of Creative Cloud comes with numerous benefits that enhance the overall user experience and productivity:

1. Access to Latest Features and Updates:

- Subscribers always have access to the latest features and updates as soon as they are released. Adobe regularly updates its software to improve performance, add new capabilities, and ensure compatibility with the latest operating systems and hardware.

2. Cloud Storage and Syncing:

- Creative Cloud subscriptions include cloud storage (ranging from 100GB to 1TB depending on the plan) for saving and accessing files from anywhere. This feature also allows for seamless syncing of settings and assets across multiple devices, ensuring consistency in your work environment.

3. Integration with Other Adobe Apps:

- Creative Cloud apps are designed to work together seamlessly. For instance, you can import and edit Illustrator files directly in InDesign or enhance images in Photoshop and use them in your InDesign projects. This tight integration streamlines workflows and increases efficiency.

4. Adobe Fonts and Adobe Stock:

- Subscribers get access to Adobe Fonts, which includes thousands of high-quality fonts that can be used in any Creative Cloud application. Additionally, Adobe Stock offers a vast library of stock photos, illustrations, and templates, which can be licensed and used in your projects.

5. Collaboration and Sharing:

- Creative Cloud offers collaboration tools that allow team members to work together on projects in real-time. Features like Share for Review enable designers to share their work with clients or colleagues and receive feedback directly within the app.

6. Learning Resources:

- Adobe provides a wealth of learning resources, including tutorials, webinars, and documentation, to help users get the most out of their software. Creative Cloud subscribers also have access to Adobe Live, where they can watch live streaming sessions from professional designers and get tips and inspiration.

7. Technical Support:

- Subscribers have access to Adobe's technical support, which includes troubleshooting assistance, live chat, and phone support. Business plans include advanced support options, ensuring that teams can resolve issues quickly and efficiently.

Conclusion

Choosing the right Adobe InDesign subscription plan depends on your specific needs, whether you're an individual creative professional, part of a business team, or a student. Understanding the various pricing options, benefits, and available discounts can help you make an informed decision. Adobe's commitment to continuous improvement and integration within the Creative Cloud ecosystem ensures that subscribers have access to the best tools and resources for their creative projects. With options for free trials, student discounts, and comprehensive support, Adobe InDesign remains an accessible and valuable tool for designers and publishers alike.

V. INSTALLATION METHOD AND REQUIREMENTS

Installing Adobe InDesign requires careful attention to system requirements and following specific steps to ensure a smooth installation process. This guide covers the system requirements for installing InDesign, a step-by-step installation guide, and troubleshooting common installation issues.

System Requirements for Installing InDesign

Before installing Adobe InDesign, it's crucial to ensure that your computer meets the necessary system requirements to run the software efficiently. Here are the minimum and recommended system requirements for Adobe InDesign 2024:

For Windows:

- **Operating System:**

    - Minimum: Microsoft Windows 10 (64-bit) version 1909 or later

    - Recommended: Microsoft Windows 11 (64-bit)

- **Processor:**

    - Minimum: Intel Pentium 4 or AMD Athlon 64 processor

    - Recommended: Intel Core i5 or AMD Ryzen 5 or higher

- **RAM:**

    - Minimum: 4GB of RAM

    - Recommended: 16GB of RAM

- **Hard Disk Space:**

    - Minimum: 3.6GB of available hard-disk space for installation; additional free space required during installation (cannot install on removable flash storage devices)

    - Recommended: SSD with 20GB of available space for optimal performance

- **Monitor Resolution:**

    - Minimum: 1024x768 display

    - Recommended: 1920x1080 or higher

- **GPU:**

  - Optional: GPU with DirectX 12 support for GPU Performance feature

For macOS:

- **Operating System:**

  - Minimum: macOS 11.0 (Big Sur) or later

  - Recommended: macOS 13.0 (Ventura) or later

- **Processor:**

  - Minimum: Multicore Intel processor with 64-bit support or Apple Silicon

  - Recommended: Intel Core i5 or Apple M1 chip or higher

- **RAM:**

  - Minimum: 4GB of RAM

  - Recommended: 16GB of RAM

- **Hard Disk Space:**

  - Minimum: 3.5GB of available hard-disk space for installation; additional free space required during installation (cannot install on a volume that uses a case-sensitive file system or on removable flash storage devices)

  - Recommended: SSD with 20GB of available space for optimal performance

- **Monitor Resolution:**

  - Minimum: 1024x768 display

  - Recommended: 1920x1080 or higher with Retina display support

How to Install InDesign

Installing Adobe InDesign involves downloading the Creative Cloud application, signing in with your Adobe ID, and managing the installation through Creative Cloud. Here is a detailed guide:

Step 1: Download the Creative Cloud Application

1. **Visit the Adobe Creative Cloud Website:**

   - Go to Adobe Creative Cloud using your web browser.

2. **Download the Creative Cloud Installer:**

   - Click on the "Download" button to download the Creative Cloud installer for your operating system (Windows or macOS).

3. **Run the Installer:**

   - Locate the downloaded installer file (usually in your Downloads folder) and double-click to run it.

4. **Follow On-Screen Instructions:**

   - Follow the on-screen instructions to complete the installation of the Creative Cloud application.

Step 2: Sign In to Creative Cloud

1. **Launch Creative Cloud:**

   - Once installed, launch the Creative Cloud application from your desktop or applications folder.

2. **Sign In with Your Adobe ID:**

   - Enter your Adobe ID (email address) and password to sign in. If you don't have an Adobe ID, you can create one by clicking the "Create an account" link.

Step 3: Install Adobe InDesign

1. **Find InDesign in Creative Cloud:**

   - In the Creative Cloud desktop application, navigate to the "Apps" tab. You will see a list of available Adobe applications.

2. **Install InDesign:**

   - Locate Adobe InDesign in the list and click the "Install" button next to it. The Creative Cloud application will begin downloading and installing InDesign.

3. **Monitor Installation Progress:**

   - You can monitor the installation progress in the Creative Cloud application. Once the installation is complete, you will see the "Open" button next to InDesign.

Steps to Take to Download and Install InDesign

1. Preparing Your System:

- **Check System Requirements:** Ensure your computer meets the minimum system requirements.

- **Backup Important Data:** It's always a good practice to back up important data before installing new software.

- **Free Up Disk Space:** Ensure you have enough free disk space for the installation.

2. Downloading InDesign:

- **Internet Connection:** Ensure you have a stable internet connection for downloading the Creative Cloud installer and InDesign.

- **Adobe Account:** Make sure you have your Adobe ID credentials ready. You'll need these to sign in and manage your Adobe subscriptions.

3. Installing InDesign:

- **Run the Installer:** After downloading, run the installer and follow the on-screen instructions.

- **Sign In:** Use your Adobe ID to sign in to the Creative Cloud application.

- **Install InDesign:** From the Creative Cloud app, select InDesign and click "Install."

4. Post-Installation Steps:

- **Launch InDesign:** After installation, launch InDesign to verify the installation was successful.

- **Update Preferences:** Set up your preferences and workspace layout according to your workflow.

- **Check for Updates:** Ensure that InDesign is updated to the latest version. You can do this from within the Creative Cloud application.

Troubleshooting Common Installation Issues

Even with a smooth installation process, you might encounter some issues. Here are common installation problems and how to resolve them:

1. Installation Fails or Hangs:

- **Solution:** Ensure your internet connection is stable. Try restarting your computer and reinstalling Creative Cloud. If the problem persists, use the Adobe Creative Cloud Cleaner Tool to remove any corrupted files and then reinstall.

2. Insufficient Disk Space:

- **Solution:** Free up disk space by deleting unnecessary files or moving them to an external drive. Check for hidden files and temporary files that can be removed.

3. Compatibility Issues:

- **Solution:** Verify that your operating system is up to date and meets the system requirements. If you're using an older OS version, consider upgrading to a compatible version.

4. Adobe ID and Sign-In Problems:

- **Solution:** Double-check your Adobe ID credentials. If you've forgotten your password, use the "Forgot password" link to reset it. Ensure that your Adobe ID is verified and active.

5. Network Issues:

- **Solution:** Ensure you have a stable and fast internet connection. If you're on a corporate network, check if there are any firewall or proxy settings blocking the download.

6. Installation Error Codes:

- **Solution:** Note the error code and search for it on the Adobe Help Center website. Adobe provides detailed solutions for specific error codes.

7. Conflicting Software:

- **Solution:** Temporarily disable antivirus software and other security programs that might interfere with the installation. Re-enable them after the installation is complete.

8. Permissions Issues:

- **Solution:** Run the installer as an administrator. On Windows, right-click the installer and select "Run as administrator." On macOS, ensure you have administrative privileges.

Conclusion

Installing Adobe InDesign involves ensuring your system meets the necessary requirements, downloading and installing the Creative Cloud application, and following the specific steps to install InDesign. By understanding the system requirements, following the step-by-step guide, and knowing how to troubleshoot common issues, you can ensure a smooth installation process. Adobe's resources and support can also provide additional help if needed, ensuring you can start creating professional-quality layouts and designs with Adobe InDesign.

VI. DESIGN CONCEPT AND MINDSET

Understanding Design Principles

Effective design relies on a deep understanding of fundamental principles that guide the creation of visually appealing and functional layouts. These principles are essential for anyone working with Adobe InDesign to produce professional-quality designs. Here are the core design principles:

1. Balance:

- Balance refers to the distribution of visual elements in a design. There are two types of balance: symmetrical (formal balance) and asymmetrical (informal balance). Symmetrical balance involves mirroring elements on either side of a central axis, creating a sense of stability. Asymmetrical balance uses different elements of varying visual weights to achieve a dynamic yet balanced composition.

2. Contrast:

- Contrast is used to create visual interest and draw attention to key elements. It involves differences in color, size, shape, and texture. High contrast can highlight important information, while low contrast can create a more harmonious and subtle design.

3. Emphasis:

- Emphasis involves creating a focal point in your design to draw the viewer's attention. This can be achieved through contrast, color, size, and placement. Emphasizing certain elements helps guide the viewer through the content in a logical and engaging way.

4. Alignment:

- Alignment ensures that elements in a design are visually connected and aligned with each other. Proper alignment creates order and organization, making the design more readable and aesthetically pleasing. It helps in creating a clean and professional look.

5. Repetition:

- Repetition involves using the same or similar elements throughout the design to create consistency and unity. It helps reinforce the overall theme and enhances the visual experience. Repeating colors, fonts, and shapes can tie different parts of a design together.

6. Proximity:

- Proximity refers to the spatial relationship between elements. Grouping related items together creates a connection between them and improves organization. It helps the viewer quickly understand and navigate the design.

7. White Space:

- White space (or negative space) is the empty space around and between elements in a design. It is crucial for preventing clutter and allowing the design to breathe. Proper use of white space improves readability and focus.

Creative Mindset and Approach

Having a creative mindset is essential for effective design. It involves approaching projects with an open mind, willingness to experiment, and a readiness to solve problems creatively. Here's how to cultivate a creative mindset:

1. Stay Curious:

- Always be curious about new design trends, techniques, and tools. Explore different styles and study the work of other designers to gather inspiration. Curiosity drives innovation and keeps your designs fresh and exciting.

2. Embrace Experimentation:

- Don't be afraid to try new ideas and take risks. Experimenting with different layouts, color schemes, and typography can lead to unique and creative solutions. Allow yourself to make mistakes and learn from them.

3. Develop a Problem-Solving Attitude:

- Design is about solving visual and communication problems. Approach each project with the mindset of finding the best solution to convey the message effectively. Analyze the problem, brainstorm ideas, and iterate until you find the best design solution.

4. Keep Learning:

- The design field is constantly evolving, and continuous learning is essential. Take online courses, attend workshops, read design books, and follow industry blogs. Keeping your skills updated will enhance your creativity and adaptability.

5. Seek Feedback:

- Feedback from peers, mentors, and clients is invaluable. It provides different perspectives and helps you improve your work. Be open to constructive criticism and use it to refine your designs.

Importance of Consistency and Branding

Consistency and branding are critical components of successful design. They ensure that your designs are cohesive and reinforce the brand identity effectively.

1. Consistency:

- Consistency in design refers to the uniform use of elements such as colors, fonts, and layout styles across all materials. It creates a cohesive look and feel, making it easier for the audience to recognize and engage with your content. Consistency builds trust and professionalism.

2. Branding:

- Branding involves creating a distinct identity for a product, service, or company. It includes elements like logos, color schemes, typography, and imagery that represent the brand's personality and values. Effective branding helps differentiate a brand from its competitors and fosters a strong connection with the audience.

3. Design Systems:

- Developing a design system or style guide is essential for maintaining consistency and branding. A design system includes guidelines for colors, fonts, icons, and other design elements. It ensures that all team members and stakeholders use the same standards, resulting in cohesive and aligned designs.

4. Brand Voice:

- Consistent branding extends beyond visuals to include the brand's voice and messaging. Ensure that the tone, style, and messaging align with the brand's identity across all communications. This consistency strengthens brand recognition and loyalty.

Practical Tips for Beginners

For beginners using Adobe InDesign, here are some practical tips to help you get started and create effective designs:

1. Learn the Basics:

- Start with the fundamentals of InDesign, such as understanding the workspace, tools, and basic functions. Adobe offers comprehensive tutorials and resources that cover the essentials.

2. Use Templates:

- Utilize InDesign templates to kickstart your projects. Templates provide a solid foundation and help you understand the structure and layout of professional designs. Customize templates to suit your needs and gradually learn how to create your own from scratch.

3. Master Typography:

- Typography is a crucial element in design. Learn about different fonts, how to pair them, and how to use character and paragraph styles in InDesign. Good typography enhances readability and visual appeal.

4. Practice Layout Design:

- Experiment with different layout designs to understand the principles of alignment, proximity, and white space. Practice creating grids and guides to help you structure your designs effectively.

5. Explore Color Theory:

- Understanding color theory is essential for creating harmonious designs. Learn about color schemes, the psychology of colors, and how to apply them in your designs. Use InDesign's color tools to experiment with different palettes.

6. Stay Organized:

- Keep your InDesign projects organized by using layers, naming conventions, and folder structures. This will make it easier to manage complex projects and collaborate with others.

7. Utilize Creative Cloud Libraries:

- Take advantage of Adobe Creative Cloud Libraries to store and access your design assets. Libraries allow you to save colors, styles, images, and more, ensuring consistency across projects.

8. Get Inspired:

- Look for inspiration from various sources such as design portfolios, magazines, and online platforms like Behance and Dribbble. Analyzing and deconstructing the work of experienced designers can provide valuable insights and spark new ideas.

9. Seek Feedback and Iterate:

- Don't hesitate to share your work with peers, mentors, or online communities. Constructive feedback helps you improve and refine your designs. Be open to suggestions and continuously iterate on your work.

10. Practice, Practice, Practice:

- The more you practice, the more proficient you will become. Work on personal projects, participate in design challenges, and take on freelance work to apply your skills in real-world scenarios.

Conclusion

Adopting a design mindset and understanding the fundamental principles of design are crucial for creating effective and visually appealing layouts in Adobe InDesign. By cultivating a creative approach, emphasizing consistency and branding, and following practical tips, beginners can develop their skills and produce professional-quality designs. Continuous learning, experimentation, and seeking feedback are key to mastering InDesign and advancing in the field of design.

VII. FUTURE USE OF ADOBE INDESIGN

Adobe InDesign remains a cornerstone tool in the graphic design industry, continually evolving to meet the needs of modern designers. As the design landscape shifts, InDesign is poised to adapt and grow with emerging trends and innovations. Here, we explore the future use of Adobe InDesign by examining the latest trends in graphic design, upcoming features and innovations, and strategies for adapting to industry changes.

Emerging Trends in Graphic Design

1. Interactive and Immersive Content:

- The demand for interactive content is rising, driven by the need for engaging user experiences. InDesign's capabilities for creating interactive PDFs and digital publications will become increasingly important. Designers are expected to integrate multimedia elements such as video, audio, animations, and interactive forms to captivate audiences.

2. Augmented Reality (AR) and Virtual Reality (VR):

- AR and VR are transforming the way we interact with digital content. InDesign will likely incorporate features that allow designers to create layouts and assets optimized for AR and VR environments. This includes 3D modeling support and the ability to design immersive experiences directly within the platform.

3. Personalized and Data-Driven Design:

- Personalization in design, driven by data analytics, is becoming more prevalent. InDesign can integrate with data sources to create customized content tailored to individual preferences. This trend will enhance marketing efforts by producing targeted and relevant materials.

4. Minimalist and Sustainable Design:

- The minimalist design trend focuses on simplicity and functionality, emphasizing clean lines, ample white space, and limited color palettes. Sustainability in design involves using eco-friendly materials and practices. InDesign will support these trends by providing tools for efficient, low-impact design processes.

5. Advanced Typography:

- Typography continues to evolve, with designers experimenting with variable fonts, custom typefaces, and advanced typographic layouts. InDesign's robust typography tools will be crucial for implementing these innovative text treatments, allowing for more expressive and unique designs.

6. Remote Collaboration:

- The rise of remote work has increased the need for collaborative design tools. InDesign will likely enhance its cloud-based features to facilitate real-time collaboration, version control, and seamless communication among design teams working from different locations.

Innovations and Upcoming Features

Adobe consistently updates InDesign with new features and enhancements to keep pace with industry demands. Here are some anticipated innovations and features:

1. AI and Machine Learning Integration:

- Adobe Sensei, Adobe's AI and machine learning platform, is expected to play a larger role in InDesign. Future updates may include AI-powered design suggestions, automated layout adjustments, and intelligent asset management. These features will help streamline the design process and boost productivity.

2. Enhanced Digital Publishing Tools:

- InDesign's digital publishing capabilities will continue to expand, offering more robust tools for creating eBooks, digital magazines, and interactive content. Features like responsive design for various devices, enhanced HTML export options, and improved interactivity will be key focus areas.

3. Cloud-Based Enhancements:

- Adobe Creative Cloud integration will become more seamless, with improved cloud storage, asset sharing, and collaboration tools. Users can expect features like real-time co-editing, more powerful Creative Cloud Libraries, and integrated review workflows to enhance team collaboration.

4. Augmented Reality Tools:

- As AR becomes more mainstream, InDesign may introduce tools for designing AR experiences. This could include capabilities for creating and visualizing AR content, such as interactive posters and brochures that come to life through AR applications.

5. Advanced Typography Features:

- Future updates will likely enhance InDesign's typography tools, supporting new font technologies and advanced text manipulation options. Variable fonts, for instance, allow designers to create dynamic and responsive text that adapts to different contexts and devices.

6. Integration with Other Adobe Tools:

- InDesign's interoperability with other Adobe Creative Cloud applications will continue to improve. Enhanced integration with Photoshop, Illustrator, After Effects, and Adobe XD will streamline workflows, allowing designers to move seamlessly between different tools and leverage their combined strengths.

Adapting to Industry Changes

To stay competitive and relevant in the ever-evolving design industry, designers must be adaptable and proactive in embracing new trends and technologies. Here are strategies for adapting to industry changes with Adobe InDesign:

1. Continuous Learning and Skill Development:

- Stay updated with the latest InDesign features and industry trends by participating in online courses, webinars, and workshops. Adobe provides a wealth of learning resources, including tutorials and certification programs, to help designers enhance their skills.

2. Embrace New Technologies:

- Experiment with new technologies such as AR, VR, and AI to stay ahead of the curve. Incorporate these technologies into your design projects to create innovative and engaging content. Familiarize yourself with tools and plugins that extend InDesign's capabilities in these areas.

3. Focus on User Experience:

- Prioritize user experience in your designs by creating interactive and immersive content. Use InDesign's interactive features to develop engaging digital publications that offer a rich user experience. Pay attention to usability and accessibility to ensure your designs are inclusive and user-friendly.

4. Collaborate and Network:

- Leverage InDesign's collaboration tools to work effectively with team members and clients. Participate in design communities, forums, and social media groups to network with other designers, share knowledge, and stay informed about industry developments.

5. Streamline Workflows:

- Optimize your design workflows by using InDesign's productivity features such as master pages, styles, and Creative Cloud Libraries. Automate repetitive tasks and create templates to save time and maintain consistency across projects.

6. Stay Flexible:

- Be open to change and willing to adapt your design approach based on new trends and client needs. Experiment with different design styles and techniques to expand your creative repertoire and stay versatile.

7. Focus on Sustainability:

- Incorporate sustainable design practices into your workflow by choosing eco-friendly materials, reducing waste, and designing with longevity in mind. Use InDesign's tools to create efficient and sustainable layouts that minimize environmental impact.

Conclusion

The future of Adobe InDesign is bright, with continuous innovations and updates that keep it at the forefront of graphic design software. By understanding emerging trends, leveraging upcoming features, and adapting to industry changes, designers can maximize the potential of InDesign and stay competitive in the dynamic design landscape. Continuous learning, embracing new technologies, and focusing on user experience and sustainability are key strategies for thriving in the future of graphic design with Adobe InDesign.

VIII. CAREER OPPORTUNITIES WITH INDESIGN

Adobe InDesign is a powerful tool for creating professional-quality layouts and designs, making it an essential skill for many roles in the design and publishing industries. Understanding the career opportunities available for InDesign users can help you chart a path to a successful and fulfilling career. This guide covers various roles and professions utilizing InDesign, tips for building a portfolio, the pros and cons of freelancing versus in-house design, and strategies for networking and professional growth.

Roles and Professions Utilizing InDesign

Adobe InDesign is used in a wide range of roles and industries. Here are some of the key positions that require proficiency in InDesign:

1. Graphic Designer:

- Graphic designers use InDesign to create visually appealing layouts for print and digital media. This includes designing brochures, posters, business cards, advertisements, and social media graphics. They combine text, images, and other design elements to communicate messages effectively.

2. Layout Artist:

- Layout artists specialize in arranging text and images in a visually pleasing and organized manner. They work on magazines, newspapers, books, and other publications, ensuring that each page layout is consistent and visually appealing.

3. Art Director:

- Art directors oversee the visual aspects of a project, from concept to completion. They use InDesign to create and manage design elements, ensuring that all visual components align with the project's vision and brand guidelines. Art directors often lead a team of designers and provide creative direction.

4. Print Designer:

- Print designers focus on creating materials that will be physically printed, such as packaging, labels, stationery, and marketing collateral. They use InDesign to design and prepare files for print production, ensuring high-quality output.

5. Publication Designer:

- Publication designers work on books, magazines, newspapers, and other printed media. They use InDesign to create layouts that enhance readability and visual appeal, often working closely with editors and writers to integrate text and images seamlessly.

6. Marketing and Communications Specialist:

- Marketing and communications specialists use InDesign to create promotional materials, such as flyers, brochures, newsletters, and email campaigns. They ensure that all marketing collateral is visually appealing and aligns with the brand's identity.

7. UX/UI Designer:

- While primarily focused on digital interfaces, UX/UI designers can use InDesign to create wireframes, mockups, and prototypes for websites and mobile applications. InDesign's interactive features allow designers to demonstrate how users will interact with digital products.

8. Freelance Designer:

- Freelance designers offer their design services to various clients on a project basis. Proficiency in InDesign allows them to take on a wide range of projects, from print materials to digital content, and work independently.

9. Production Artist:

- Production artists focus on the technical aspects of design, ensuring that files are correctly prepared for printing or digital distribution. They use InDesign to make final adjustments, check for errors, and ensure that designs meet production specifications.

Building a Portfolio

A strong portfolio is essential for showcasing your skills and landing job opportunities. Here are some tips for building an impressive InDesign portfolio:

1. Curate Your Best Work:

- Select your best and most relevant projects to include in your portfolio. Quality is more important than quantity, so choose pieces that demonstrate your skills and creativity effectively.

2. Showcase a Range of Projects:

- Include a variety of projects that highlight your versatility. Show different types of work, such as brochures, posters, magazines, and digital publications, to demonstrate your ability to handle diverse design challenges.

3. Highlight Your Process:

- Include case studies that explain your design process, from concept to final product. Describe the problem you were solving, your approach, and the tools and techniques you used. This helps potential employers understand your thinking and problem-solving abilities.

4. Include Personal Projects:

- If you're just starting and don't have many client projects, include personal projects in your portfolio. These can showcase your creativity, passion, and initiative.

5. Keep It Updated:

- Regularly update your portfolio with new work. Remove outdated or less impressive pieces to keep your portfolio fresh and relevant.

6. Create a Professional Presentation:

- Ensure your portfolio is well-organized and visually appealing. Use InDesign to create a digital portfolio or a PDF that you can share with potential clients or employers. You can also create an online portfolio using platforms like Behance or Adobe Portfolio.

Freelancing vs. In-House Design

Both freelancing and in-house design careers have their pros and cons. Here's a comparison to help you decide which path might be right for you:

Freelancing:

Pros:

- **Flexibility:** Freelancers have the freedom to choose their projects, set their schedules, and work from anywhere.

- **Diverse Projects:** Freelancers often work with various clients, providing opportunities to work on different types of projects and industries.

- **Potential for Higher Earnings:** Successful freelancers can potentially earn more than in-house designers, especially if they build a strong client base and charge premium rates.

Cons:

- **Income Instability:** Freelancing can be unpredictable, with fluctuating income and periods of no work.

- **Self-Management:** Freelancers must manage all aspects of their business, including finding clients, marketing, billing, and handling taxes.

- **Lack of Benefits:** Freelancers do not receive benefits such as health insurance, paid time off, or retirement plans.

In-House Design:

Pros:

- **Stability:** In-house designers have a steady paycheck, job security, and benefits such as health insurance and paid time off.

- **Collaborative Environment:** Working as part of a team provides opportunities for collaboration, mentorship, and professional development.

- **Focused Work:** In-house designers often focus on a single brand or product, allowing for a deep understanding of the brand's identity and goals.

Cons:

- **Less Flexibility:** In-house designers typically have fixed schedules and less control over their workload and project choices.

- **Potential for Monotony:** Working on the same brand or product can sometimes lead to repetitive tasks and less variety in projects.

- **Limited Earning Potential:** In-house designers usually have a fixed salary with less opportunity for significant income growth compared to successful freelancers.

Networking and Professional Growth

Building a strong professional network and continuously developing your skills are crucial for career advancement. Here are some strategies for networking and professional growth:

1. Join Professional Organizations:

- Join design organizations such as AIGA (American Institute of Graphic Arts), which offer networking opportunities, resources, and events. Membership can provide access to industry leaders, job boards, and professional development programs.

2. Attend Industry Events:

- Attend conferences, workshops, and meetups to connect with other professionals in the field. Events like Adobe MAX offer valuable learning opportunities and the chance to network with peers and industry experts.

3. Leverage Social Media:

- Use platforms like LinkedIn, Twitter, and Instagram to connect with other designers, share your work, and stay updated on industry trends. Participating in online design communities can also help you build relationships and gain exposure.

4. Seek Mentorship:

- Find a mentor who can provide guidance, support, and valuable insights into the industry. Mentors can help you navigate your career path, improve your skills, and expand your network.

5. Continue Learning:

- Invest in your professional development by taking online courses, attending workshops, and reading design books and blogs. Staying current with the latest design trends and software updates is essential for staying competitive.

6. Collaborate on Projects:

- Collaborate with other designers on personal or professional projects. Collaboration can lead to new ideas, skill development, and opportunities for future partnerships.

7. Build an Online Presence:

- Create a strong online presence by maintaining a professional website and portfolio. Share your work on platforms like Behance, Dribbble, and Adobe Portfolio to reach a wider audience and attract potential clients or employers.

8. Participate in Design Competitions:

- Enter design competitions to showcase your skills and gain recognition. Winning or being shortlisted in a competition can boost your credibility and provide valuable exposure.

Conclusion

Adobe InDesign opens up numerous career opportunities in the design and publishing industries. By understanding the various roles that utilize InDesign, building a strong portfolio, deciding between freelancing and in-house design, and actively networking and pursuing professional growth, you can build a successful and fulfilling career. Whether you choose to work independently or as part of a team, continuous learning and adapting to industry changes will ensure that you remain competitive and thrive in your design career.

CHAPTER 2: KEYBOARD SHORTCUTS IN INDESIGN

Keys for tools

Result	Windows	Mac OS
Temporarily select Selection or Direct Selection tool (last used)	Any tool (except selection tools)+Ctrl	Any tool (except selection tools)+ Command
Temporarily select Group Selection tool	Direct Selection tool+Alt; or Pen, Add Anchor Point, or Delete Anchor Point tool+Alt+Ctrl	Direct Selection tool+Option; or Pen, Add Anchor Point, or Delete Anchor Point tool+Option+Command
Select container of selected content	Esc or double-click	Esc or double-click
Select content of selected container	Shift+Esc or double-click	Shift+Esc or double-click
Add to or subtract from a selection of multiple objects	Selection, Direct Selection, or Group Selection tool+Shift–click (to deselect, click center point)	Selection, Direct Selection, or Group Selection tool+Shift–click (to deselect, click center point)
Duplicate selection	Selection, Direct Selection, or Group Selection tool+Alt–drag*	Selection, Direct Selection, or Group Selection tool+ Option–drag*
Duplicate and offset selection	Alt+Left Arrow, Right Arrow, Up Arrow, or Down Arrow key	Option+Left Arrow, Right Arrow, Up Arrow, or Down Arrow key
Duplicate and offset selection by 10 times**	Alt+Shift+Left Arrow, Right Arrow, Up Arrow, Down Arrow key	Option+Shift+Left Arrow, Right Arrow, Up Arrow, Down Arrow key
Move selection**	Left Arrow, Right Arrow, Up Arrow, Down Arrow key	Left Arrow, Right Arrow, Up Arrow, Down Arrow key
Move selection by 10th**	Ctrl+Shift+Left Arrow, Right Arrow, Up Arrow, Down arrow key	Command+Shift+Left Arrow, Right Arrow, Up Arrow, Down arrow key
Move selection by 10 times**	Shift+Left Arrow, Right Arrow, Up Arrow, Down Arrow key	Shift+Left Arrow, Right Arrow, Up Arrow, Down Arrow key
Select parent page item from document page	Selection or Direct Selection tool+Ctrl+Shift–click	Selection or Direct Selection tool+Command+Shift–click
Select next object behind or in front	Selection tool+Ctrl–click, or Selection tool+Alt+Ctrl–click	Selection tool+Command–click or Selection tool+Option+ Command–click
Select next or previous frame in story	Alt+Ctrl+Page Down/ Alt+Ctrl+Page Up	Option+Command+Page Down/ Option+Command+Page Up
Select first or last frame in story	Shift+Alt+Ctrl+Page Down/ Shift+Alt+Ctrl+Page Up	Shift+Option+Command+Page Down/ Shift+Option+Command+Page Up
*Press Shift to constrain movement to 45° angles.		
**Amount is set in Edit > Preferences > Units & Increments (Windows) or InDesign > Preferences > Units & Increments (Mac OS).		

Keys for transforming objects

Result	Windows	Mac OS
Duplicate and transform selection	Transformation tool+Alt–drag*	Transformation tool+Option–drag*
Display Transform tool dialog box	Select object+double-click Scale tool, Rotate tool, or Shear tool in Toolbox	Select object+double-click Scale tool, Rotate tool, or Shear tool in Toolbox
Decrease scale by 1%	Ctrl+,	Command+,
Decrease scale by 5%	Ctrl+Alt+,	Command+Option+,
Increase scale by 1%	Ctrl+.	Command+.

Increase scale by 5%	Ctrl+Alt+.	Command+Option+.
Resize frame and content	Selection tool+Ctrl–drag	Selection tool+Command–drag
Resize frame and content proportionately	Selection tool+Shift+Ctrl–drag	Selection tool+Shift+Command–drag
Constrain proportion	Ellipse tool, Polygon tool, or Rectangle tool+Shift–drag	Ellipse tool, Polygon tool, or Rectangle tool+Shift–drag
Switch image from High Quality Display to Fast Display	Ctrl+Alt+Shift+Z	Command+Option+Shift+Z

*After you select a transformation tool, hold down the mouse button, and then hold down Alt (Windows) or Option (Mac OS) and drag. Press Shift to constrain movement to 45° angles.

Keys for editing paths and frames

Result	Windows	Mac OS
Temporarily select Convert Direction Point tool	Direct Selection tool+Alt+Ctrl, or Pen tool+Alt	Direct Selection tool+Option+ Command, or Pen tool+Option
Temporarily switch between Add Anchor Point and Delete Anchor Point tool	Alt	Option
Temporarily select Add Anchor Point tool	Scissors tool+Alt	Scissors tool+Option
Keep Pen tool selected when pointer is over path or anchor point	Pen tool+Shift	Pen tool+Shift
Move anchor point and handles while drawing	Pen tool+spacebar	Pen tool+spacebar
Display the Stroke panel	F10	Command+F10

Keys for tables

Result	Windows	Mac OS
Insert or delete rows or columns while dragging	Begin dragging row or column border, and then hold down Alt as you drag	Begin dragging row or column border, and then hold down Option as you drag
Resize rows or columns without changing the size of the table	Shift–drag interior row or column border	Shift–drag interior row or column border
Resize rows or columns proportionally	Shift–drag right or bottom table border	Shift–drag right or bottom table border
Move to next/previous cell	Tab/Shift+Tab	Tab/Shift+Tab
Move to first/last cell in column	Alt+Page Up/ Alt+Page Down	Option+Page Up/ Option+Page Down
Move to first/last cell in row	Alt+Home/ Alt+End	Option+Home/ Option+End
Move to first/last row in frame	Page Up/Page Down	Page Up/Page Down
Move up/down one cell	Up Arrow/Down Arrow	Up Arrow/Down Arrow
Move left/right one cell	Left Arrow/Right Arrow	Left Arrow/Right Arrow
Select cell above/below the current cell	Shift+Up Arrow/ Shift+Down Arrow	Shift+Up Arrow/ Shift+Down Arrow
Select cell to the right/left of the current cell	Shift+Right Arrow/ Shift+Left Arrow	Shift+Right Arrow/ Shift+Left Arrow
Start row on next column	Enter (numeric keypad)	Enter (numeric keypad)
Start row on next frame	Shift+Enter (numeric keypad)	Shift+Enter (numeric keypad)
Toggle between text selection and cell selection	Esc	Esc

Keys for finding and changing text

Result	Windows	Mac OS
Insert selected text into Find What box	Ctrl+F1	Command+F1
Insert selected text into Find What box and finds next	Shift+F1	Shift+F1
Find next occurrence of Find What text	Shift+F2 or Alt+Ctrl+F	Shift+F2 or Option+Command+F
Insert selected text into Change To box	Ctrl+F2	Command+F2
Replace selection with Change To text	Ctrl+F3	Command+F3

Keys for working with type

Result	Windows	Mac OS
Bold (only for fonts with bold face)	Shift+Ctrl+B	Shift+Command+B
Italic (only for fonts with italic face)	Shift+Ctrl+I	Shift+Command+I
Normal	Shift+Ctrl+Y	Shift+Command+Y
Underline	Shift+Ctrl+U	Shift+Command+U
Strikethrough	Shift+Ctrl+/	Control+Shift+Command+/
All caps (on/off)	Shift+Ctrl+K	Shift+Command+K
Asian language hyphenation	Shift+Ctrl+K	Shift+Command+K
Small caps (on/off)	Shift+Ctrl+H	Shift+Command+H
Tate-chu-yoko setting	Shift+Ctrl+H	Shift+Command+H
Superscript	Shift+Ctrl+(+) [plus sign]	Shift+Command+(+) [plus sign]
Subscript	Shift+Alt+Ctrl+(+) [plus sign]	Shift+Option+Command+(+) [plus sign]
Reset horizontal or vertical scale to 100%	Shift+Ctrl+X or Shift+Alt+Ctrl+X	Shift+Command+X or Shift+Option+Command+X
Basic letter group setting or detail setting	Shift+Ctrl+X or Shift+Alt+Ctrl+X	Shift+Command+X or Shift+Option+Command+X
Align left, right, or center	Shift+Ctrl+L, R, or C	Shift+Command+L, R, or C
Justify all lines	Shift+Ctrl+F (all lines) or J (all but last line)	Shift+Command+F (all lines) or J (all but last line)
Align both ends or equal spacing	Shift+Ctrl+F (align both end) or J (equal spacing)	Shift+Command+F (align both ends) or J (equal spacing)
Increase or decrease point size*	Shift+Ctrl+> or <	Shift+Command+> or <
Increase or decrease point size by five times*	Shift+Ctrl+Alt+> or <	Shift+Command+ Option+> or <
Increase or decrease leading (horizontal text)*	Alt+Up Arrow/ Alt+Down Arrow	Option+Up Arrow/ Option+Down Arrow
Increase or decrease leading (vertical text)*	Alt+Right Arrow/ Alt+Left Arrow	Option+Right Arrow/ Option+Left Arrow
Increase or decrease leading by five times (horizontal text)*	Alt+Ctrl+Up Arrow/ Alt+Ctrl+Down Arrow	Option+Command+Up Arrow/ Option+Command+Down Arrow
Increase or decrease leading by five times (vertical text)*	Alt+Ctrl+Right Arrow/ Alt+Ctrl+Left Arrow	Option+Command+Right Arrow/ Option+Command+Left Arrow
Auto leading	Shift+Alt+Ctrl+A	Shift+Option+Command+A
Align to grid (on/off)	Shift+Alt+Ctrl+G	Shift+Option+Command+G
Auto-hyphenate (on/off)	Shift+Alt+Ctrl+H	Shift+Option+Command+H
Increase or decrease kerning and tracking (horizontal text)	Alt+Left Arrow/Alt+Right Arrow	Option+Left Arrow/ Option+Right Arrow
Increase or decrease kerning and tracking (vertical text)	Alt+Up Arrow/ Alt+Down Arrow	Option+Up Arrow/ Option+Down Arrow

Increase or decrease kerning and tracking by five times (horizontal text)	Alt+Ctrl+Left Arrow/ Alt+Ctrl+Right Arrow	Option+Command+Left Arrow/ Option+Command+Right Arrow
Increase or decrease kerning and tracking by five times (vertical text)	Alt+Ctrl+Up Arrow/ Alt+Ctrl+Down Arrow	Option+Command+Up Arrow/ Option+Command+Down Arrow
Increase kerning between words*	Alt+Ctrl+\	Option+Command+\
Decrease kerning between words*	Alt+Ctrl+Backspace	Option+Command+Delete
Clear all manual kerning and reset tracking to 0	Alt+Ctrl+Q	Option+Command+Q
Increase or decrease baseline shift** (horizontal text)	Shift+Alt+Up Arrow/ Shift+Alt+Down Arrow	Shift+Option+Up Arrow/ hift+Option+Down Arrow
Increase or decrease baseline shift** (vertical text)	Shift+Alt+Right Arrow/ Shift+Alt+Left Arrow	Shift+Option+Right Arrow/ Shift+Option+Left Arrow
Increase or decrease baseline shift by five times (horizontal text)	Shift+Alt+Ctrl+Up Arrow/ Shift+Alt+Ctrl+Down Arrow	Shift+Option+Command+Up Arrow/ Shift+Option+Command+Down Arrow
Increase or decrease baseline shift by five times (vertical text)	Shift+Alt+Ctrl+Right Arrow/ Shift+Alt+Ctrl+Left Arrow	Shift+Option+Command+Right Arrow/ hift+Option+Command+Left Arrow
Automatically flow story	Shift–click loaded text icon	Shift–click loaded text icon
Semi-automatically flow story	Alt–click loaded text icon	Option–click loaded text icon
Recompose all stories	Alt+Ctrl+/	Option+Command+/
Insert current page number	Shift+Alt+Ctrl+N	Shift+Option+Command+N

*Press Shift to increase or decrease kerning between words by five times.
**Amount is set in Edit > Preferences > Units & Increments (Windows) or InDesign > Preferences > Units & Increments (Mac OS).

Keys for navigating through and selecting text

Result	Windows	Mac OS
Move to right or left one character	Right Arrow/ Left Arrow	Right Arrow/ Left Arrow
Move up or down one line	Up Arrow/ Down Arrow	Up Arrow/ Down Arrow
Move to right or left one word	Ctrl+Right Arrow/ Ctrl+Left Arrow	Command+Right Arrow/ Command+Left Arrow
Move to start or end of line	Home/End	Home/End
Move to previous or next paragraph	Ctrl+Up Arrow/ Ctrl+Down Arrow	Command+Up Arrow/ Command+Down Arrow
Move to start or end of story	Ctrl+Home/ Ctrl+End	Command+Home/ Command+End
Select one word	Double-click word	Double-click word
Select one character right or left	Shift+Right Arrow/ Shift+Left Arrow	Shift+Right Arrow/ Shift+Left Arrow
Select one line above or below	Shift+Up Arrow/ Shift+Down Arrow	Shift+Up Arrow/ Shift+Down Arrow
Select start or end of line	Shift+Home/ Shift+End	Shift+Home/ Shift+End
Select one paragraph	Triple-click or quadruple-click paragraph, depending on Text Preferences setting	Triple-click or quadruple-click paragraph, depending on Text Preferences setting
Select one paragraph before or after	Shift+Ctrl+Up Arrow/ Shift+Ctrl+Down Arrow	Shift+Command+Up Arrow/ Shift+Command+Down Arrow
Select current line	Shift+Ctrl+\	Shift+Command+\
Select characters from insertion point	Shift–click	Shift–click

Select start or end of story	Shift+Ctrl+Home/ Shift+Ctrl+End	Shift+Command+Home/ Shift+Command+End
Select all in story	Ctrl+A	Command+A
Select first/last frame	Shift+Alt+Ctrl+Page Up/ Shift+Alt+Ctrl+Page Down	Shift+Option+ Command+Page Up/ Shift+Option+ Command+Page Down
Select previous/next frame	Alt+Ctrl+Page Up/ Alt+Ctrl+Page Down	Option+Command+Page Up/ Option+Command+Page Down
Delete word in front of insertion point (Story Editor)	Ctrl+Backspace or Delete	Command+Delete or Del (numeric keypad)
Update missing font list	Ctrl+Alt+Shift+/	Command+Option+Shift+/

Keys for viewing documents and document workspaces

Result	Windows	Mac OS
Temporarily select Hand tool	Spacebar (with no text insertion point), Alt-drag (with text insertion point), or Alt+spacebar (in both text and non-text modes)	Spacebar (with no text insertion point), Option–drag (with text insertion point), or Option+spacebar (in both text and nontext modes)
Temporarily select **Zoom In** tool	Ctrl+spacebar	Command+spacebar
Temporarily select **Zoom Out** tool	Alt+Ctrl+spacebar or Alt+**Zoom In** tool	Option+Command+spacebar or Option+**Zoom In** tool
Zoom to 50%, 200%, or 400%	Ctrl+5, 2, or 4	Command+5, 2, or 4
Redraw screen	Shift+F5	Shift+F5
Open new default document	Ctrl+Alt+N	Command+Option+N
Switch between current and previous zoom levels	Alt+Ctrl+2	Option+Command+2
Switch to next/previous document window	Ctrl+~ [tilde]/ Shift+Ctrl+F6 or Ctrl+Shift+~ [tilde]	Command+F6 or Command+~ [tilde]/ Command+Shift+~ [tilde]
Scroll up/down one screen	Page Up/Page Down	Page Up/Page Down
Go back/forward to last-viewed page	Ctrl+Page Up/ Ctrl+Page Down	Command+Page Up/ Command+Page Down
Go to previous/next spread	Alt+Page Up/ Alt+Page Down	Option+Page Up/ Option+Page Down
Fit spread in window	Double-click Hand tool	Double-click Hand tool
Activate the Go To command	Ctrl+J	Command+J
Fit selection in window	Ctrl+Alt+(+) [plus sign]	Command+Option+(+) [plus sign]
Display the entire object	Ctrl+Alt+(+) [plus sign]	Command+Option+(+) [plus sign]
Go to parent page while Pages panel is closed	Ctrl+J, type prefix of parent, press Enter	Command+J, type prefix of parent, press Return
Cycle through units of measurement	Shift+Alt+Ctrl+U	Shift+Option+Command+U
Snap guide to ruler increments	Shift–drag guide	Shift–drag guide
Switch between page and spread guides (creation only)	Ctrl–drag guide	Command–drag guide

		Control-drag object
Temporarily turn on/off snap to		Control-drag object
Create vertical and horizontal ruler guides for the spread	Ctrl–drag from zero point	Command–drag from zero point
Select all guides	Alt+Ctrl+G	Option+Command+G
Lock or unlock zero point	Right-click zero point and choose an option	Control–click zero point and choose an option
Use current magnification for view threshold of new guide	Alt–drag guide	Option–drag guide
Select buttons in alert dialog boxes	Press first letter of button name, if underlined	Press first letter of button name
Show information on installed plug-ins and InDesign components	Ctrl+Help > About Design	Command+InDesign menu > About InDesign

Keys for working with XML

Result	Windows	Mac OS
Expand/Collapse element	Right Arrow/Left Arrow	Right Arrow/Left Arrow
Expand/Collapse element and child elements	Alt+Right Arrow/ Alt+Left Arrow	Option+Right Arrow/ Option+Left Arrow
Extend XML selection up/down	Shift+Up Arrow/ Shift+Down Arrow	Shift+Up Arrow/ Shift+Down Arrow
Move XML selection up/down	Up Arrow/ Down Arrow	Up Arrow/ Down Arrow
Scroll structure pane up/down one screen	Page Up/ Page Down	Page Up/ Page Down
Select first/last XML node	Home/ End	Home/ End
Extend selection to first/last XML node	Shift+Home/ Shift+End	Shift+Home/ Shift+End
Go to previous/next validation error	Ctrl+Left Arrow/ Ctrl+Right Arrow	Command+Left Arrow/ Command+Right Arrow
Automatically tag text frames and tables	Ctrl+Alt+Shift+F7	Command+Option+Shift+F7

Keys for indexing

Result	Windows	Mac OS
Create index entry without dialog box (alphanumeric only)	Shift+Ctrl+Alt+[	Shift+Command+Option+[
Open index entry dialog box	Ctrl+7	Command+7
Create proper name index entry (last name, first name)	Shift+Ctrl+Alt+]	Shift+Command+Option+]

Keys for panels

Result	Windows	Mac OS
Delete without confirmation	Alt-click Delete icon	Option-click Delete icon
Create item and set options	Alt-click New button	Option-click New button
Apply value and keep focus on option	Shift+Enter	Shift+Enter

Activate last-used option in last-used panel	Ctrl+Alt+~ [tilde]	Command+Option+~ [tilde]
Select range of styles, layers, links, swatches, or library objects in a panel	Shift-click	Shift-click
Select nonadjacent styles, layers, links, swatches, or library objects in a panel	Ctrl-click	Command-click
Apply value and select next value	Tab	Tab
Move focus to selected object, text, or window	Esc	Esc
Show/Hide all panels, Toolbox, and Control panel (with no insertion point)	Tab	Tab
Show/Hide all panels except the Toolbox and Control panel (docked or not)	Shift+Tab	Shift+Tab
Open or close all stashed panels	Ctrl+Alt+Tab	Command+Option+Tab
Stash a panel group	Alt+drag any panel tab (in the group) to edge of screen	Option+drag any panel tab (in the group) to edge of window
Select item by name	Alt+Ctrl-click in list, and then use keyboard to select item by name	Option+Command-click in list and then use keyboard to select item by name
Open the Drop Shadow panel	Alt+Ctrl+M	Command+Option+M

Keys for the Control panel

Result	Windows	Mac OS
Toggle focus to/from Control panel	Ctrl+6	Command+6
Toggle Character/Paragraph text attributes mode	Ctrl+Alt+7	Command+Option+7
Change reference point when proxy has focus	Any key on the numeric keypad or keyboard numbers	Any key on the numeric keypad or keyboard numbers
Display the pop-up menu that has focus	Alt+Down Arrow	
Open Units & Increments Preferences	Alt-click Kerning icon	Option-click Kerning icon
Open the Text Frame Options dialog box	Alt-click Number Of Columns icon	Option-click Number of Columns icon
Open the Move dialog box	Alt-click X or Y icon	Option-click X or Y icon
Open the Rotate dialog box	Alt-click Angle icon	Option-click Angle icon
Open the Scale dialog box	Alt-click X or Y Scale icon	Option-click X or Y Scale icon
Open the Shear dialog box	Alt-click Shear icon	Option-click Shear icon
Open Text Preferences	Alt-click Superscript, Subscript, or Small Caps button	Option-click Superscript, Subscript, or Small Caps button
Open the Underline Options dialog box	Alt-click Underline button	Option-click Underline button

Open the Strikethrough Options dialog box	Alt-click Strikethrough button	Option-click Strikethrough button
Open the Grids Preferences	Alt-click Align To Baseline Grid, or Do Not Align To Baseline Grid button	Option-click Align To Baseline Grid, or Do Not Align To Baseline Grid button
Open the Drop Caps & Nested Styles dialog box	Alt-click Drop Cap Number Of Lines, or Drop Cap One Or More Characters icon	Option-click Drop Cap Number Of Lines, or Drop Cap One Or More Characters icon
Open the Justification dialog box	Alt-click Leading icon	Option-click Leading icon
Open Named Grid dialog box	Double-click Named Grid icon	Double-click Named Grid icon
Open New Named Grid Options dialog box	Alt-click Named Grid icon	Option-click Named Grid icon
Open Frame Grid Options dialog box	Alt-click Number of characters Horizontal, Number of Characters Vertical, Character Aki, Line Aki, Vertical Scale, Horizontal Scale, Grid View, Font Size, Number of Columns, or Column Gutter icon	Option-click Number of characters Horizontal, Number of Characters Vertical, Character Aki, Line Aki, Vertical Scale, Horizontal Scale, Grid View, Font Size, Number of Columns, or Column Gutter icon

Keys for type panels and dialog boxes

Result	Windows	Mac OS
Open Justification dialog box	Alt+Ctrl+Shift+J	Option+Command+Shift+J
Open Paragraph Rules dialog box	Alt+Ctrl+J	Option+Command+J
Open Keep Options dialog box	Alt+Ctrl+K	Option+Command+K
Activate Character panel	Ctrl+T	Command+T
Activate Paragraph panel	Ctrl+Alt+T	Command+Option+T

Keys for the character and paragraph styles

Result	Windows	Mac OS
Make character style definition match text	Select text and press Shift+Alt+Ctrl+C	Select text and press Shift+Option+Command+C
Make paragraph style definition match text	Select text and press Shift+Alt+Ctrl+R	Select text and press Shift+Option+Command+R
Change options without applying style	Shift+Alt+Ctrl-double-click style	Shift+Option+Command-double-click style
Remove style and local formatting	Alt-click paragraph style name	Option-click paragraph style name
Clear overrides from paragraph style	Alt+Shift-click paragraph style name	Option+Shift-click paragraph style name
Show/hide Paragraph and Character Styles panels, respectively	F11, Shift+F11	Command+F11, Command+Shift+F11

Keys for the Tabs panel

Result	Windows	Mac OS
Activate Tabs panel	Shift+Ctrl+T	Shift+Command+T
Switch between alignment options	Alt-click tab	Option-click tab

Keys for the Layers panel

Result	Windows	Mac OS
Select all objects on layer	Alt-click layer	Option-click layer
Copy selection to new layer	Alt-drag small square to new layer	Option-drag small square to new layer
Add new layer below selected layer	Ctrl-click Create New Layer	Command-click Create New Layer
Add new layer to the top of the layer list	Shift+Ctrl-click Create New Layer	Shift+Command-click Create New Layer
Add new layer to the top of the layer list and open New Layer dialog box	Shift+Alt+Ctrl-click Create New Layer	Cmd+Option+Shift-click Create New Layer
Add new layer and open New Layer dialog box	Alt-click Create New Layer	Option-click Create New Layer

Keys for the Pages panel

Result	Windows	Mac OS
Apply parent to selected page	Alt-click parent	Option-click parent
Base another parent page on selected parent	Alt-click the parent you want to base the selected parent on	Option-click the parent you want to base the selected parent on
Create parent page	Ctrl-click Create New Page button	Command-click Create New Page button
Display Insert Pages dialog box	Alt-click New Page button	Option-click New Page button
Add new page after last page	Shift+Ctrl+P	Shift+Command+P

Keys for the Color panel

Result	Windows	Mac OS
Move color sliders in tandem	Shift-drag slider	Shift-drag slider
Select a color for the nonactive fill or stroke	Alt-click color bar	Option-click color bar
Switch between color modes (CMYK, RGB, LAB, HSB)	Shift-click color bar	Shift-click color bar

Keys for using the Separations Preview panel

Result	Windows	Mac OS
Turn on Overprint preview	Ctrl+Alt+Shift+Y	Command+Option+Shift+Y
Show all plates	Ctrl+Alt+Shift+~ [tilde]	Command+Option+Shift+~ [tilde]
Show Cyan plate	Ctrl+Alt+Shift+1	Command+Option+Shift+1
Show Magenta plate	Ctrl+Alt+Shift+2	Command+Option+Shift+2
Show Yellow plate	Ctrl+Alt+Shift+3	Command+Option+Shift+3
Show Black plate	Ctrl+Alt+Shift+4	Command+Option+Shift+4
Show 1st Spot plate	Ctrl+Alt+Shift+5	Command+Option+Shift+5
Show 2nd Spot plate	Ctrl+Alt+Shift+6	Command+Option+Shift+6
Show 3rd Spot plate	Ctrl+Alt+Shift+7	Command+Option+Shift+7

Keys for the Swatches panel

Result	Windows	Mac OS
Create new swatch based on the current swatch	Alt-click New Swatch button	Option-click New Swatch button

Create spot color swatch based on the current swatch	Alt+Ctrl-click New Swatch button	Option+Command-click New Swatch button
Change options without applying swatch	Shift+Alt+Ctrl-double-click swatch	Shift+Option+Command-double-click swatch

Keys for the Transform panel

Result	Windows	Mac OS
Apply value and copy object	Alt+Enter	Option+Enter
Apply width, height, or scale value proportionally	Ctrl+Enter	Command+Enter

Keys for resolving conflicts between Mac OS 10.3x and 10.4

Result	Mac OS
Open Preferences dialog box	Command+K
Open Paragraph Styles panel	Command+F11
Open Character Styles panel	Command+Shift+F11
Open Swatches panel	F5
Open Pages panel	Command+F12
Minimize active application window	Command+M
Hide application	Command+H

CHAPTER 3: OPTIMIZING YOUR WORKSPACE

WORKSPACE OVERVIEW

Some of the Adobe Creative Cloud apps, like InDesign, have user interface features like panels, bars, and windows that make it easier to create and handle documents. The way these things are set up and arranged together makes up what is called a "workspace." Workspaces give users a planned and well-organized place to quickly find their way around an app's features and tools. The goal is to improve user efficiency and make processes more efficient.

KEY ELEMENTS OF WORKSPACES

1. **Panels, Bars, and Windows**: Workspaces are made up of important interface elements like panels, bars, and windows that are arranged in a way that helps with different program tasks and functions.

2. **Consistent Appearance**: Workspaces have the same look, so they are all the same in different parts of the program. This choice in design makes things easier for the user and makes it simple to switch between tasks or functions.

3. **Customization Options**: Users can change their workspaces to fit their tastes and ways of working. This customization can include moving panels around, changing the layout, or making some parts less or more visible.

Home Screen

When you open InDesign for the first time or when there are no documents open, the Home screen is the first thing that you see. It gives users quick access to important features like tutorials, options for creating documents, and the ability to open projects that have already been saved.

Customization

- Users can modify their workspace by choosing from pre-set options made for specific tasks or by making their unique setups. Individuals can tailor their surroundings to their particular wants and working styles thanks to their flexibility.

These tabs and buttons are on the Home screen:

- **New file**: To create a new document, click this button. One of the many templates and presets that are available in InDesign can be used to create a document.

- **Open**: Click this button to open an existing document in InDesign.

- **Home**: Click this tab to see the most recent changes you made to files.

- **Learn**: InDesign lessons for beginners and experts can be found on this tab. Clicking on it will bring up a list of courses.

Note: To turn off the Home screen in the Preferences menu, go to Preferences > General and uncheck the box next to Show Home Screen When No Documents Are Open. It is still possible to use the keyboard keys Ctrl/Cmd + O and Ctrl/Cmd + N.

WORKSPACE OVERVIEW

InDesign's workspace lets you change how the windows, panels, and tools are laid out, so you can make your own unique design area.

A. Tabbed Document windows B. Workspace switcher C. Search bar with autocomplete suggestions D. Panel title bar E. Collapse to Icons button F. Panel groups in vertical dock G. Status bar H. Tools panel

Application Frame

- The Application frame is a window that connects all the parts of the Adobe InDesign area so that they work well together as a single unit. The design of this frame keeps things from clashing, and it can be adjusted quickly when the size or position is changed. Panels inside the Application frame can be seen even when you switch to or click on something outside of the application. People who are working with more than one program can put them next to each other or on different computers. Through the Window menu on macOS, you can turn on or off the standard user interface.

Application Bar

- The desktop switcher, menus (only in Windows), and other program settings are in the Application bar, which runs across the top. When the Application frame is off on macOS, you can get to the application bar. The Window menu gives users the freedom to turn it on or off as needed.

Tools Panel

- The Tools panel is an important part that has many tools for making and editing pictures, artwork, and page elements. The functionality of the tools is used to organize them sensibly, making them easier to find and more efficient for users.

Control Panel

- The Control panel shows options that are related to the currently chosen item, making it easy for users to get to the setup settings. This makes updating easier by making sure that the right options are always close at hand.

Document Window

- The Document window is where the user works with the file most of the time. It shows what's in the text and can have windows that are grouped or sorted. Document windows can be grouped and docked in some situations to make them easier to find.

Panels

- Adobe InDesign's panels are a great way to keep an eye on work and make changes to it. Users can arrange them in any way they like—grouped, stacked, or docked. Panels make it easier to get to different functions, tools, and information, which make the area more efficient overall.

CHANGE SCREEN MODES

To change how visible the document window is, go to View > Screen Mode. When the toolbar is in a single column, click the "current mode" button to get to the menu where you can pick from different modes.

- **Normal Mode**: Shows artwork in a normal window with all lines and guides visible, as well as items that aren't being printed and a white board.

- **Preview Mode**: Shows artwork as if it were printed, hiding all parts that aren't needed for printing (like grids, guides, and objects that aren't needed for printing) and setting the pasteboard's background color to the preview color set in Preferences.

- **Bleed Mode**: This mode shows the artwork as if it were printed, hiding any elements that aren't needed for printing (like grids, guides, and objects that aren't needed for printing). The pasteboard is set to the preview background color chosen in Preferences, and any printing elements within the document's bleed area (set in Document Setup) are shown.

- **Slug Mode**: In slug mode, it displays artwork as if it were printed with all non-printing elements (like grids, guides, and non-printing objects) hidden, the pasteboard is set to the preview background color set in Preferences, and any printing elements within the document's slug area (set in Document Setup) are shown.

- **Presentation Mode**: ▢ This mode shows the artwork as if it were a slideshow presentation, with no choices, panels, or tools visible.

Use the status bar

In Adobe InDesign, the progress bar in the lower-left corner of the document window is useful for getting information about the file and making it easier to move between pages. Users can use its menu to do different things, which makes their work easier and helps them keep track of their files.

Menu Options

1. **Reveal in File System (Windows) or Finder (macOS):**

   - On Windows, you can use the "Reveal in Explorer" option in the status bar menu to show the file in the file system.

   - The same thing can be done on macOS by pressing "Reveal in Finder." This option starts the Finder and shows where the file is stored in the file system.

2. **Reveal in Adobe Bridge:**

   - To open Adobe Bridge and find the file, users can choose "Reveal in Bridge" from the menu in the status bar. This option makes it easier to integrate with Adobe Bridge so that you can handle your files better.

Note on Zoom Percentage Display

- On macOS, users can show the zoom percentage in the status bar by removing the application bar. The "Application Bar" can be turned on and off by going to the "Window" menu and picking "Application Bar."

- However, Windows users can't hide the application bar in Adobe InDesign like macOS users can.

All of these menu options and extra features make the Adobe InDesign experience more complete and easier to use. They make it easier to handle files, move between pages, and change how they see things based on their operating system.

CONTROL PANEL OVERVIEW

The Control panel, which you can get to by going to Window > Control, is a flexible and adaptable tool in Adobe InDesign that makes it easy to get to options, instructions, and related panels for certain page items. The Control panel is initially docked at the top, but users can change its location by docking it at the bottom, turning it into a moving panel, or hiding it completely.

Key Features and Options

- **Frames**: The Control panel's option to scale, move, tilt, spin, or apply object styles is available when working with frames. This gives you a central place to change different frame characteristics within the text.

- **Text**: The Control panel shows word or phrase options for text-related choices. To quickly switch between these options, users can click on the items on the left side of the Control panel. This makes it easier to change the characteristics of text based on certain needs.

- **Tables**: The Control panel has options to change the size, join rows, arrange text, and add lines when working with tables. This specific set of tools makes it easy to customize tables, which improves the user experience when working with tabular material.

Tooltips and Additional Information

- Additionally, users can get more information about each option in the Control panel by using Tooltips. This is because the options change depending on what is chosen. Tooltips are short instructions that show up when you move the finger over an icon or option name. This function helps give people relevant knowledge and direction.

Opening Dialog Boxes

- The Alt + Click (Windows) or Option + Click (macOS) keyboard shortcut can be used to open dialog boxes that are linked to Control panel buttons. The quick switch to thorough settings and setups for certain options is made possible by this feature.

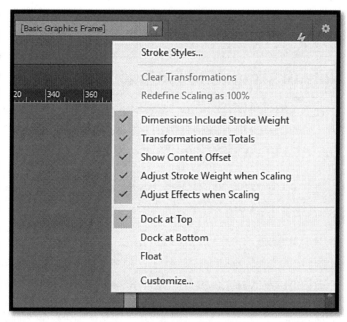

The flexible and context-aware options in the Control panel, along with its combination with Tooltips, make Adobe InDesign's design environment more efficient and easier to use. Because it puts settings for different page features in one place, it makes the workflow smoother and makes design tasks easier and more accurate.

WORKSPACE CONFIGURATION

Managing Windows and Panels in Adobe InDesign

For a customizable and streamlined Adobe InDesign process, you need to be able to manage document windows and panels well. You are free to make your own work spaces, move windows, and change the way panels look however you like. You can also save these personalized workspaces so they are easy to get to when you need them.

Creating Custom Workspaces

1. **Customizing Windows**:

   - Move and change the positions of document windows to make a layout that works for you.

   - Open more than one file at once. If the Document windows are tabbed, you can move them around by dragging the tab of one window to a different spot in the group.

2. **Docking Document Windows**: Docking includes putting Document windows in a group. To move a window into a different group of Document windows, just drag it into the group you want.

3. **Undocking (Floating or Untabbing) Document Windows**: By dragging the tab of a Document window out of the group, you can undock the window from the group. This lets the window move on its own or stops being linked.

Saving Custom Workspaces

- Once you've set up the document windows and screens the way you want, you can save the custom workspace to use again later.

- Go to Window > Workspace > New Workspace to save a workspace. Give your custom workspace a name and pick which parts of it to include, like document windows, menu arrangements, and so on. To save, click OK.

Switching Between Workspaces

- The unique workspaces you've saved can be easily switched between once you've saved them. Select the Workspace you want from the list by going to Window > Workspace.

You can change your Adobe InDesign workspace to fit your tasks and tastes if you learn how to handle windows and panels in this way. This level of customizing makes you more productive by making sure that the documents and tools you need are easy to find and set up in a way that fits your routine.

DOCK AND UNDOCK PANELS

When you use Adobe InDesign, a dock is a group of panels or panel groups that are shown together, usually vertically. Users can make their workspace fit their needs by docking and undocking panels.

This makes it easy to get to the tools and functions they need. This is how you can manage panels in a dock:

- **Docking a Panel**: To dock a single panel, grab it by its tab and drag it to where you want it to be. Docks can be put between panels, at the top, or the bottom.

- **Docking a Panel Group**: Panel groups with multiple tabs can be docked by dragging the full group into the dock using the title bar (the solid, empty bar above the tabs).

- **Removing a Panel or Panel Group**: When you want to get rid of a panel or panel group from the dock, drag it out by its tab or title bar. You can let it float on its own or move it to a different dock by doing this.

- **Customization Tips**: You can move panels around in a dock to make it work better for you. For instance, putting together pieces that do the same thing can make them work better.

Overall Steps

1. **Docking a Panel**:

   - First, grab it by its tab.

   - Drag it to where you want it to dock (at the top, bottom, or between other panels).

2. **Docking a Panel Group**:

   - Grab the title bar of the whole panel group.

   - Move the group to the dock by dragging it there.

3. **Removing a Panel or Panel Group**:

   - Drag it out of the dock by its tab or title bar.

   - You can let it float on its own or drop it into another dock.

Hide or show all panels

- Press **Tab** to show or hide all panels, even the **Tools** and **Control** panels.

- Press **Shift+Tab** to show or hide all windows except the **Tools** and **Control** panels.

Add, remove, and move panels

If you take away all of a dock's panels, the dock goes away. By moving panels to the right edge of the workspace until a drop zone shows up, you can make a dock.

- If you want to add a panel, choose it from the **Window** menu and put it where you want it.

- To get rid of a panel, right-click on its tab (Windows) or control-click on it (macOS) and choose **Close**.

- Drag a panel by its tab to move it.

- Drag the title bar to move a panel group.

Note: The drop zone is activated by where the mouse is placed, not where the panel is placed. If you can't see the drop zone, try moving the mouse to where it should be.

Stack floating panels

A panel floats easily when you drag it out of its dock, but it doesn't go into a drop zone. With the floating panel, you can put it anywhere in the workspace. You can stack floating panels or groups of panels so that when you drag the title bar at the top, they move together.

- Drag a panel by its tab to the drop zone at the bottom of another panel to stack them.

- Drag a panel up or down by its tab to change how it stacks.

Collapse and expand panel icons

To make the workspace less crowded, you can shrink panels to icons. Some of the time, windows are folded into icons in the default workspace.

- Click the **>>** button at the top of the dock to make all the panel icons in a column collapse or expand. To make an icon in a single panel bigger, pick it.

- Change the width of the dock to change the size of panel buttons and hide titles for a cleaner look. Expand the dock to see the words on the icons.

- You can move panel icons around in the dock, between docks, or as floating icons by dragging them.

SCALE THE USER INTERFACE

InDesign's **User Interface Scaling** can be changed to fit your needs. When you open InDesign with new preferences, it figures out what size screen you have and changes the application's scaling factor to fit.

These steps will help you change the size of the user interface on your screen:

1. For Windows, go to **Edit > Preferences > User Interface**. For macOS, go to **InDesign > Preferences > User Interface**.

2. Choose the **UI Sizing** slider to change the UI's size based on your screen resolution.

There is a sample of the scaled UI next to the slider that you can look at.

1. Choose the **Scale Cursor Proportionately** option to make the cursor buttons the right size for the screen.

2. Use the slider to change the size of the **Anchor Points**, the **handle**, and the **Box Bounding Display Size**.

3. Startup InDesign again to use the new settings. The changes will be made the next time you open InDesign, even if you don't restart it now.

CREATE AND SWITCH WORKSPACES

You can easily get back to the current panel size and position by making a named workspace and saving it. This works even if panels are closed or moved. The workspace switcher in the application bar shows the names of saved workspaces.

1. Go to **Window > Workspace > New Workspace** and give the workspace a name.

2. Pick one or more of the following options under **Capture**:

- **Panel Locations**: This item saves where the panels are now (currently).

- **Menu Customization**: It saves the current set of menus.

Reset and delete workspaces

- To change a workspace, go to **Windows > Workspace > Reset <Workspace name>**.

- Go to **Windows > Workspace > Delete Workspace** to get rid of a workspace.

Toolbox overview

You can choose, change, and make new page parts with some of the tools in the toolbox. You can pick out types, forms, lines, and colors with other tools. You can change how the toolbox is laid out overall to suit how you like your windows and panels to be set up. By default, the toolbox shows up as a single set of tools going up and down. On top of that, you can make it into a double column or a single row. However, you can't change where different tools are located in the toolbox. You can move the toolbox by dragging its top. Click on a tool in the default toolbox to choose it.

There are also some hidden tools in the toolbox that are tied to the ones that can be seen. Arrows to the right of the tool buttons show you which tools are hidden. To get to a hidden tool, click and hold the tool you want to use in the toolbox, and then pick out the hidden tool. When you move the mouse over a tool, the name of the tool and its keyboard shortcut shows up. This text is called the "tool tip." You can disable tooltips by picking "None" from the ToolTips menu in the Interface settings. **Note**: To see what shortcuts and control keys work with the chosen tool, go to **Window > Utilities > Tool Hints** and open the Tool Hints panel.

A Selection tools

- ▶ **Selection (V, Escape)***
- ▶ **Direct Selection (A)**
- ▶ **Page (Shift + P)**
- |↔| **Gap (U)**
- ▦ **Content Collector (B)**
  - ▦ Content Placer

B Drawing and Type tools

- T **Type (T)**
  - ↗ Type On a Path (Shift+T)
- ╲ **Line (\)**
- ✎ **Pen (P)**
  - ✎⁺ Add Anchor Point (=)
  - ✎⁻ Delete Anchor Point (-)
  - ⌐ Convert Direction Point (Shift+C)
- ✐ **Pencil (N)**
  - ✐ Smooth
  - ✐ Erase
- ⊠ **Rectangle Frame (F)**
  - ⊗ Ellipse Frame
  - ⊗ Polygon Frame
- ▭ **Rectangle (M)**
  - ◯ Ellipse (L)
  - ◯ Polygon

C Transformation tools

- ✄ **Scissors (C)**
- ▦ **Free Transform (E)**
  - ↻ Rotate (R)
  - ▦ Scale (S)
  - ▱ Shear (O)
- ▬ **Gradient Swatch (G)**
- ▦ **Gradient Feather (Shift+G)**

D Modification and Navigation tools

- ▤ **Note**
- ⚲ **Eyedropper (I)**
  - ⁄ Measure (K)
- ✋ **Hand (H)**
- 🔍 **Zoom (Z)**

- **Display the toolbox**: Go to **Window > Tools**.

- **Display tool options**: First, double-click a tool in the list of tools.

- The Eyedropper, Pencil, and Polygon tools are some of the tools that this procedure works for.

Display and select hidden tools

1. Place the mouse over a tool in the toolbox that has secret tools and hold down the mouse button.

2. Pick a tool when the hidden tools show up.

Select tools temporarily

1. First, choose a tool and hold down the shortcut key for a different tool.

2. Perform an action while holding down the keyboard shortcut.

3. Let go of the keyboard shortcut to go back to the previous tool.

For instance, hold down the V key while the Gap tool is chosen to use the Selection tool for a short time. The Gap tool is chosen when you let go of the V key.

View tool hints

The Tool Hints panel tells you how to use the modifier keys with the current tool.

1. To see the Tool Hints panel, go to **Window > Utilities > Tool Hints**.

2. Click on a tool in the toolbox to see a list of its modifier keys and methods to use it.

Change the toolbox layout

1. To change the interface, go to **Edit > Preferences > Interface** (Windows) or **InDesign > Preferences > Interface** (Mac OS).

2. From the menu in the Floating Tools Panel, pick a layout option and click **OK**.

To change how the toolbox is laid out, you can also click the double arrow icon at the top of it.

PREFERENCES AND SETTINGS

Adjusting preferences in Adobe InDesign is a crucial step in tailoring the software to meet your specific needs. Let's delve into the process of customizing general preferences for an enhanced user experience.

1. **Accessing Preferences**:

- On Windows, navigate to **Edit > Preferences > General**.

- On macOS, go to **InDesign > Preferences > General**, and then choose your desired preference type.

2. **Page Numbering**:

- Explore the "View" menu under "Page Numbering" to select a preferred method for numbering pages.

3. **Font Downloading and Embedding**:

- Determine the font subsetting level based on the number of characters in the Font Downloading and Embedding area. This setting influences font options in Print and Export dialog boxes.

4. **Scaling Preferences**:

- Customize how scaled items are displayed in panels and how the content of scaled frames behaves in the "When Scaling" area.

  - Opt for "Apply to Content" to adjust the point size when resizing a text frame. When applied to a graphics frame, the image's percentage size changes while the frame's percentage size remains at 100%.
  - Choose "Adjust Scaling Percentage" to view the old and new point sizes side by side during text scaling. Scaling a graphics frame alters both the frame and the image's percentage size.

5. **Resetting Warning Dialogs**:

- Click the "Reset All Warning Dialogs" button to reset all warnings, including those previously marked not to show. This ensures that all warnings are visible, allowing you to make informed decisions about each one.

By configuring these general preferences, you can streamline your workflow and make Adobe InDesign align more closely with your specific requirements. These adjustments pave the way for a more personalized and efficient design experience.

Document preview

In Windows' File Explorer and macOS' Finder, you can see previews of your InDesign documents. Not able to see the preview? To add or change the preview settings, do these things:

1. **Accessing File Handling Preferences**:

- On Windows, navigate to **Edit > Preferences > File Handling**.

- On macOS, go to **InDesign > Preferences > File Handling**.

2. **Always Save Preview Images with Documents**:

- Mark the checkbox labeled "Always Save Preview Images with Documents." This ensures that preview images are consistently saved along with your documents.

3. **Choosing Text Settings**:

  - Under the Text Settings section, make selections based on your preferences:

    - **Pages**: Choose from options like First Page, First 2 Pages, First 5 Pages, First 10 Pages, or All Pages to specify which pages you want to save as previews. The default is usually the First 2 Pages.
    - **Preview Size**: Opt for Small (128x128), Medium (256x256), Large (512x512), or Extra Large (1024x1024) to determine the size of the preview image. The default is often Large (512x512).

4. **Applying Changes**:

  - Click the **OK** button to confirm and apply the selected file handling preferences.

CUSTOMIZE USER INTERFACE SCALING

Set up InDesign's scaling options so that the user interface is always the same size no matter what your screen resolution is. Some parts of the user interface are scaled correctly so that they look good on high-resolution devices. Once you open InDesign with new preferences, it figures out what size screen you have and changes the app's UI scale to fit. **Note**: Keep in mind that UI scaling doesn't work on low-resolution screens.

Adjusting the user interface scaling in Adobe InDesign can greatly enhance your workspace experience. Here's a simple guide on how to set the user interface scaling:

1. **For Windows Users**:

  - Navigate to **Edit > Preferences > User Interface Scaling**.

2. **For Mac Users**:

  - Go to **InDesign > Preferences > User Interface Scaling**.

To change how the Interface looks, use the following options in the User Interface Scaling dialog:

- **UI**: Use the UI size slider to change how big or small the UI is. Most of the time monitors with a better resolution need a bigger scale factor. Next to the tool is a sample of the UI that has been adjusted. To use the new settings, restart InDesign. If you decide to restart later, the changes you made will show up the next time you open InDesign. How many stops are shown in the slider depends on the resolution of your screen. For screens with better resolutions, more stops are shown.

- **Cursor**: This option makes the cursor icons the same size as the UI when it is turned on (ON by default).

- **Anchor Points, Handle, and Bounding Box Display Size**: This section lets you change the size of the anchor points, direction handles, and bounding box displays. To do this, move the slider to change the size of the displays.

Set defaults

If you make changes to the settings while no documents are open, those changes will be used for all new documents. If you make changes while a document is open, these changes will only affect that document. In the same way, if you change settings while no objects are chosen, the new objects will use those values by default.

Change default settings for new documents

1. **Close All Documents**:

   - Ensure that all open documents are closed before making any changes.

2. **Customize Menu Items, Panels, or Dialog Boxes**:

   - Make the desired modifications to menu items, panels, or dialog boxes based on your preferences.
   - Explore different settings and layouts to tailor the workspace to your specific needs.

Note: If your documents share similar characteristics (size and language), you can make these changes even when no document is open.

For example:

1. To set the usual page size, close all documents, go to **File > Document Setup**, and select your preferred page size.
2. For language preferences, close all documents, navigate to **Edit > Preferences > Dictionary** (Windows) or **InDesign > Preferences > Dictionary** (macOS), and choose an option from the Language menu to set the usual dictionary.

By customizing these defaults, you can create a personalized and efficient workspace in Adobe InDesign, enhancing your overall user experience.

Specify default settings for new objects in a document

1. **Open the Document**:

   - Launch Adobe InDesign and open the document you want to work on.

2. **Deselect All**:

   - Go to the "Edit" menu and select **Deselect All** to ensure that no specific elements or objects are currently selected.

3. **Customize Menu Items, Panels, or Dialog Boxes**:

- Make the desired changes to menu items, panels, or dialog boxes according to your preferences.
- Explore different settings and layouts to tailor the document workspace to your specific needs.

Restore all preferences and default settings

It often fixes problems with InDesign by deleting preferences, which is also called "trashing preferences" or "removing preferences." You should make a copy of the selection files called InDesign Defaults and InDesign Saved Data just in case. You don't have to delete your preferences; you can just put these backup files over the corrupted preference files and not lose any of your changes.

Follow these steps based on your OS:

Windows:

1. Open InDesign.
2. Simultaneously press **Shift + Ctrl + Alt**.
3. Confirm that you want to delete preference files when prompted by clicking "Yes."

MacOS:

1. Start InDesign.
2. Hold down **Shift + Option + Command + Control**.
3. Confirm the deletion of preference files by clicking "Yes" when prompted.

Locating Preference Files

The Adobe InDesign preference files store various program settings and choices. These files, along with the "InDesign Defaults" file, are saved upon closing InDesign. **To manually delete or rename them, navigate to the following directories**:

- **For Windows**:

    - **C:\Users\[username]\AppData\Roaming\Adobe\InDesign\[version number]\[language]**

- **For macOS**:

    - **/Users/[username]/Library/Preferences/Adobe InDesign/[version number]/[language]/**

Replace **[username]** with your actual username, **[version number]** with the version number (e.g., 15.0 or 14.0), and **[language]** with your language code (e.g., en_US or jp_JP). This process helps reset preferences, potentially resolving issues and enhancing the performance of Adobe InDesign. **Note**: Change **[version number]** to the version number of the product, such as 15.0 or 14.0. Change **[language]** to the language you want to use, such as en_US or jp_JP.

CHAPTER 4: STARTING YOUR FIRST DOCUMENT

CREATING A NEW DOCUMENT

When you use InDesign to create a document, you don't have to start with a fresh blank document. Instead, you can pick from a lot of different templates, some of which come from Adobe Stock. There are tools in templates that you can use to finish your project. You can work on a template in InDesign the same way you work on any other Adobe InDesign file. Besides using templates, you can also choose one of InDesign's many presets to start making a page.

TEMPLATES AND PRESETS

Templates

Templates give you rich, creative content that you can use again and again in your documents. You can get templates from Adobe Stock that come with high-quality pictures and graphics that you can use right in InDesign. After that, you can easily make documents that use the same settings and design by adding to these models. For common jobs like design of business cards or handouts, InDesign also offers blank templates with fixed measurements and settings. They are saved as **.indd** files in InDesign.

Blank Document Presets

Blank document Presets are new documents that already have the right size and settings. It's easy to design for certain gadget shapes or uses when you use presets. Like, you can use a preset to start creating for the iPad right away. Blank document presets have choices for size, pages, columns, alignment, placement, margins, and gaps that are already set. You can change these choices before using the preset to make a document.

These sets are what templates and presets are categorized into:

- **Print**

- **Web**

- **Mobile**

Access the New Document dialog

1. Launch InDesign

2. Do one of these things:

   - Go to **File > New**.

   - In the Start workspace, click **New** or **Start New**.

   - Press the following key combination:

- **Cmd+N** on a Mac

- **Ctrl+N** on a PC

- Right-click on the tab for an open document and then select **"New Document"** from the menu that appears.

Overview: New Document dialog

The New Document dialog box lets you do many things, such as:

- Create documents using chosen templates from Adobe Stock in several areas, such as Print, Web, and Mobile;

- Look for more templates on Adobe Stock and make documents using them;

- The Recent tab lets you quickly get to files, themes, and other things you've recently used.

- Get to templates you've downloaded from Adobe Stock quickly with the Saved tab.

- Use Blank Document presets for a variety of groups and device form factors to make documents. You can change the settings for the presets before you open them.

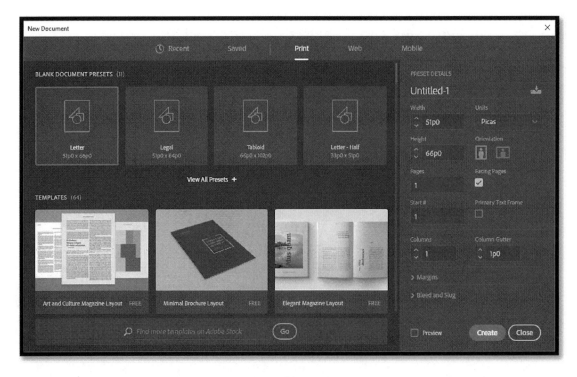

Create documents using presets

1. In the **New Document** dialog box, click on one of the tabs that say **Print**, **Web**, or **Mobile**.

2. Pick out a preset.

3. If you want to, you can change the settings for the preset you chose in the pane on the right called **"Preset Details."**

4. Click on **Create**. The preset tells InDesign to open a new document for you.

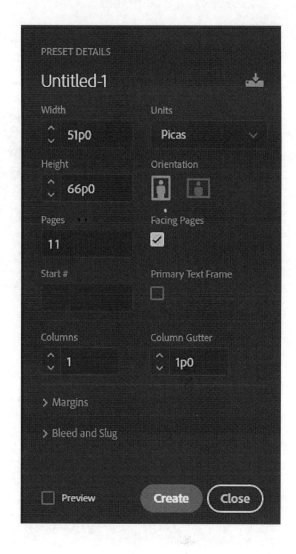

Modify presets

In the right pane, you can change the settings of a preset document before starting it.

1. Give the document a name.

2. Choose the following options for the preset that was chosen:

3. Click the **Create** button to start a new document with the preset options.

Create documents using templates from Stock

There are many templates from Adobe Stock that come with InDesign. There are templates for tablets, phones, letterheads, folders, business cards, and more. Simple fonts or fonts that can be triggered from Adobe Fonts are used in templates with font layers.

Follow these steps to make a document using a template:

1. In the **New Document** window, click on one of the tabs that say **"Print," "Web,"** or **"Mobile."**

2. Pick out a template.

3. Click **"See Preview"** to see what the style will look like. You can look at a sample, which is a picture of a template, and decide if you want to order that template.

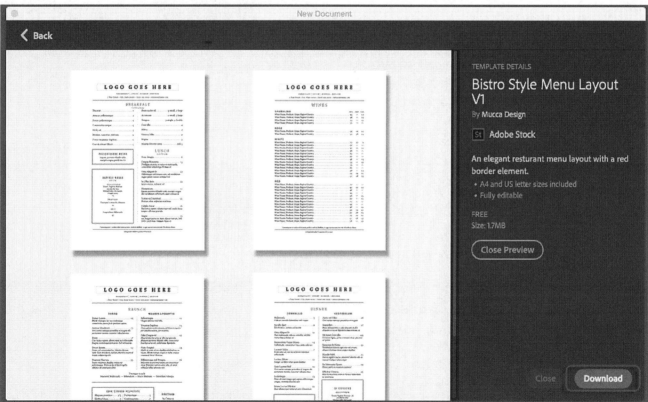

4. Click on **Download**. You are asked by InDesign to buy the template from Adobe Stock.

You can open the template as an InDesign file (.indd) to work on it after you have licensed it using resources or credits in your account.

5. Click **Open** when the file is done downloading. If you are asked to enable some fonts from Adobe Fonts when you open the template, click **OK**. Right now, you can use InDesign to work on the open file like you would any other .indd file.

Note: It's important to know that downloaded templates are added to a Creative Cloud library called **Stock Templates**. The **CC Libraries** panel is where you can find this library.

SEARCH FOR MORE TEMPLATES FROM ADOBE STOCK

Aside from the templates that come with Adobe Stock, you can also use the **New Document** window to look for and download many more of these kinds of templates.

-   Click on the **Find More Templates on Adobe Stock** box in the New Document window box and type a search word. On the other hand, you can just click **"Go"** to see all of the possible templates.

You can look around the Adobe Stock website when InDesign opens it in a new browser window. Choose the one that works best for your project and download it.

WORKING WITH PARENT PAGES

A parent page, which used to be called a master page, is like a background that you can quickly add to many pages. Things on a parent page show up on all pages that are applied to it. There are dots around parent page things that show up on document pages. When you make changes to a parent page, those changes are instantly made to pages that are linked to it. These pages usually have names, page numbers, heads, and footers that repeat. They can also have blank text or picture frames inside them that look like blank pages in a document. On a document page, you can't choose a parent item unless it is changed. In the realm of digital design, the concept of layers operates much like pages in a document, and understanding their hierarchy is crucial. Imagine layers as transparent sheets stacked on top of each other, akin to pages in a book. **Here are some key insights into working with layers**:

1. **Layer Hierarchy**:

   - Layers can be likened to different pages or levels within a document.
   - Each layer functions as an independent entity, accommodating various elements.

2. **Stacking Order**:

   - Objects within the same layer stack in a specific order. The order is vital because it determines which object appears in front when there is an overlap.
   - When two objects overlap within the same layer, the one placed later in the stacking order will appear in front.

3. **Parent Layers**:

   - Think of parent layers as master sheets that influence the content on document pages.
   - Objects on a parent layer will typically appear behind objects on the document page layer.

4. **Layer Management**:

   - To control the visibility and order of elements, layers can be managed individually.
   - Placing an object on a higher layer means it will appear behind objects on lower layers.

5. **Merging Layers**:

   - Merging layers combines them into a single entity. When this happens, objects on parent layers may be pushed behind those on document page layers.
   - It's essential to consider the layer structure before merging to avoid unintended changes in the stacking order.

Understanding the intricacies of layers is akin to mastering the art of arranging pages in a storybook. Each layer contributes to the overall composition, and manipulating their order can significantly impact the visual narrative of the design.

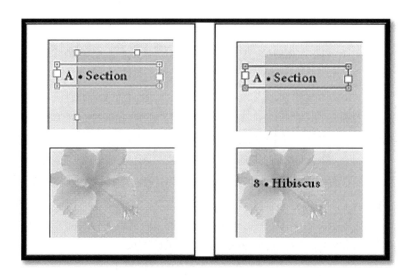

TIPS AND GUIDELINES FOR PARENT PAGES

Working with parent layers in your design not only adds versatility but also streamlines your creative process. **Here are some practical tips on harnessing the power of parent layers in your projects**:

1. **Comparing Design Ideas**:

   - Create distinct parent layers and introduce them one by one to sample pages with regular content.
   - This method allows for easy comparison of different design concepts, helping you choose the most effective visual approach.

2. **Document Templates for Efficiency**:

   - Save a set of parent layers in a document template for quick setup of new projects.
   - Your template can encompass color libraries, paragraph styles, character styles, and various presets, ensuring consistency and efficiency across different designs.

3. **Dynamic Layout Adjustments**:

   - Experiment with column and margin settings on parent layers to instantly transform the layout.
   - Adding a new parent layer with different settings dynamically adapts the content on the page, providing a swift way to explore various design possibilities.

4. **Automatic Page Numbers**:

   - When automatic page numbers are applied to a parent layer, they intelligently display the correct page numbers for each section of the document where the parent layer is utilized.
   - This feature enhances document organization and readability, particularly in multi-section projects.

Incorporating these practices into your design workflow empowers you to efficiently iterate through design variations, maintain consistency across projects, and seamlessly adapt layouts for optimal visual impact. Harness the potential of parent layers to elevate the efficiency and creativity of your design process.

Create parent pages

Understanding the default parent page in every document and its role in creating a cohesive design is crucial. **Here's a breakdown of how parent pages work and how they can simplify your design process**:

1. **Default Parent Page**:

   - Every document is equipped with a default parent page.
   - This default parent serves as the foundation for your document's layout and styling.

2. **Creating New Parents**:

- Generate new parent pages either from scratch or by deriving them from existing parent or document pages.
- This flexibility allows you to build upon established designs or start afresh, depending on your project requirements.

3. **Global Changes with Main Parent**:

- Alterations made to the main parent page automatically propagate to all document pages and other parent pages derived from it.
- This global synchronization ensures consistency across multiple sections of your document.

4. **Efficient Style Updates**:

- Planning ahead becomes a powerful strategy, enabling you to modify the style of numerous pages simultaneously.
- This efficiency is particularly valuable when dealing with extensive documents, saving time and ensuring a unified visual identity.

Create a parent from scratch

1. **Navigating to the Pages Panel**:

- To access the Pages panel, begin by opening it and then proceed to the menu section.

2. **Creating a New Parent Object**:

- Choose "New Parent" from the menu to initialize a new parent object.

3. **Customizing Parent Attributes**:

- **Input the subsequent particulars and proceed by selecting "OK"**:

    - **Prefix**: Offer a succinct prefix consisting of up to four alphanumeric characters, indicating the parent's usage for each page within the Pages panel.
    - **Name**: Allocate a descriptive title to the parent spread.
    - **Based On Parent**: Opt for an existing parent spread as a template for the new parent, or alternatively, opt for "None" to commence from a clean slate.
    - **Number of Pages**: Determine the preferred quantity of pages within the parent spread, with a maximum threshold of ten.

Create a parent from an existing page or spread

1. **Effortless Transfer Technique**:

- Within the Pages panel, smoothly relocate an entire spread from the Pages section to the Parents section.
- This user-friendly drag-and-drop maneuver promptly converts the chosen spread into a parent, simplifying the organization of your document.

2. **Save As Parent Option**:

   - Navigate to the Pages panel and choose a specific spread.
   - Opt for the "Save As Parent" option to preserve the selected spread as a designated parent.
   - Any objects present on the initial page or spread automatically become integral components of the newly created parent. If the first page utilized a parent, the new parent inherits its foundation.

Base one parent on another

Within a document, there exists the capability to craft a derivative parent version, influenced by another parent, colloquially known as the "parent parent." The components inherited from the parent parent are aptly labeled as child parents. Envision a scenario where your document comprises ten sections, each utilizing analogous parent spreads. Instead of individually adjusting each section, a more efficient approach involves the creation of a singular parent spread encompassing the shared style and elements present in all ten sections. In this context, effecting a general design modification becomes a streamlined process. A simple adjustment to the parent parent suffices, automatically applying the alterations across all ten sections. This dynamic mirrors the concept of a master template, ensuring uniformity throughout distinct segments of your document.

Furthermore, you have the flexibility to customize child parents to suit your preferences. Adjusting the parent items on a child-parent allows you to make changes to the parent, just as you would modify elements on regular document pages. This approach not only maintains a uniform design but also enables you to keep it fresh and updated easily. In the realm of desktop publishing and layout design, Adobe InDesign is a powerful tool with numerous features to enhance efficiency and creativity. One such feature involves manipulating parent spreads within the Pages panel to influence the appearance of certain elements. To make one parent look like another, follow the steps outlined below:

Method 1: Using the Pages Panel Menu

1. Launch your InDesign document.
2. Find your way to the Pages panel by opting for "Window" in the top menu and then selecting "Pages."
3. Identify the specific parent spread you intend to modify.
4. Open the Pages panel menu by clicking on the menu icon positioned in the top-right corner of the panel.
5. Within the menu, opt for "Parent Options for [parent spread name]." Substitute "[parent spread name]" with the designated name of the parent spread requiring modification.
6. In the ensuing dialog box, pinpoint the "Based On Parent" option.
7. Choose an alternative parent from the array of available options.
8. Confirm the changes by selecting "OK."

Method 2: Dragging and Dropping

1. Open your InDesign document.

2. Go to the Pages panel by selecting "Window" in the top menu and choosing "Pages."
3. Locate the parent spread you want to use as the base.
4. Click and hold on the parent's spread's name.
5. Drag the selected parent spread onto the name of another parent spread.
6. Release the mouse button to drop the parent spread.

EDIT THE LAYOUT OF A PARENT

In Adobe InDesign, manipulating the style of parent pages is a dynamic process that allows you to implement changes seamlessly across multiple pages in a document. **Here are the steps to change the style of parent pages**:

1. **Access the Parent Page**:

   - Open your InDesign document.
   - Navigate to the Pages panel by selecting "Window" in the top menu and choosing "Pages."
   - Locate the parent page button in the Pages panel.

2. **Double-Click or Choose from List**:

   - Execute a double-click on the parent page button situated within the Pages panel.
   - Alternatively, you have the option to designate the parent page by selecting it from the list of text boxes positioned at the bottom of the document window.

3. **Modify the Parent**:

   - Once the parent spread is displayed in the document box, make the necessary changes to the parent page.
   - You can add or edit text, insert images, adjust layout elements, or apply any other design modifications.

4. **Update Across Pages**:

   - Modifications applied to the parent page resonate across all pages utilizing that specific parent.
   - As an illustration, introducing text or embedding an image on the parent page manifests identical content on all pages linked to that parent.

Important Note

- It's essential to be aware that if you modify or remove a parent page object on a specific page, that object may not update to reflect changes made on the parent page.

- In other words, if you make local changes to an object on a page, it might not synchronize with the corresponding object on the parent page.

Any pages that use that parent are updated automatically by InDesign. Pick out the parent page with the Page tool, and then use the Control panel's size options to make it a different size. Utilizing multiple views in Adobe InDesign is a valuable technique to observe the effects of changes made to parent pages.

Here's how you can do it:

1. **Open Multiple Views**:

   - Navigate to the top menu and select "Window."
   - Choose "Arrange" and then select "New Window."
   - Once the new window is open, go back to "Window > Arrange" and select "Tile" to arrange the views side by side.

2. **Assign Views to Page and Parent**:

   - In one of the views, navigate to a specific page of your document that uses the parent page.
   - In the other view, navigate to the parent page itself.

3. **Make Changes to the Parent:**

   - In the view displaying the parent page, make the desired changes to the layout, text, or any other elements.

4. **Observe Changes in Page View:**

   - Switch to the view displaying the page associated with the parent.

   - As you make changes to the parent, you will observe real-time updates on the page view.

Change parent page options

1. **Select the Parent Spread:**

   - Open the Pages panel in Adobe InDesign.

   - Click on the name of the parent spread for which you want to modify the options.

2. **Access Parent Options:**

   - In the Pages panel, click on the menu icon (usually represented by three horizontal lines or a small drop-down arrow).

   - From the menu, choose "Parent Options for [parent name]." This option allows you to access and modify the settings for the selected parent spread.

3. **Modify Options:**

   - Upon initiation, a dialog box materializes, showcasing an array of options pertaining to the parent spread. Feel free to modify any preferred settings, including altering the parent's name or title, selecting an alternative parent for "Based On Parent," or fine-tuning the number of pages within the parent spread as needed.

4. **Apply Changes:**

- After making the necessary modifications, click "OK" to apply the changes.

APPLY PARENT PAGES

If your document incorporates unique layouts, such as a magazine foldout spanning three or four pages, each parent used in this context should consistently have an identical page count. Any deviation in page count may alter the size of the layout page. In cases where the parent page exhibits a distinct page size compared to the layout page, it influences the dimensions of the layout. If the layout page boasts its own customized page size, you have the option to adopt the dimensions of the parent page or maintain the layout page's specific size. It's important to take note that the periphery of parent items within a text page is delineated. There is a possibility that the parent item is concealed on a lower layer or that the parent items are hidden, rendering them imperceptible on the page. To address this, navigate to the Pages panel menu and select "Show Parent Items" to reveal any obscured elements.

Apply a parent to a document page or spread

1. **Grasp the parent page icon** and drag it onto the designated page icon within the Pages panel. Release the mouse button when a black rectangle materializes, signifying the selection of the page you intend to link with the parent.

2. **Alternatively**, if you opt to assign a parent page to an entire spread, access the Pages panel. Subsequently, drag the parent page icon to one of the corners of the spread. Release the mouse button when a black rectangle envelops all the pages within the spread that you aim to associate with the parent.

Apply a parent to multiple pages

1. **Manual Selection:**

   - Go to the Pages panel and opt for the pages you wish to associate with a new parent.
   - **Click on the desired parent while simultaneously holding down Alt (Windows) or Option (Mac OS).**

2. **Menu Option:**

   - Navigate to the Pages panel and access the menu.
   - **Choose "Apply Parent to Pages" from the menu.**
   - **Select the parent you want to apply.**
   - **Verify that the intended page groups are chosen under the "To Pages" option.**
   - **Confirm the application of the parent to the selected pages by clicking OK.**

It's worth noting that multiple pages can share the same parent simultaneously. If you want to apply the same parent to non-consecutive pages, you can use a comma-separated format (e.g., 5, 7-9, 13-16) to specify the pages you wish to include in the parent assignment. These methods provide a convenient way to efficiently manage and apply parent-child relationships to multiple pages in your document.

Unassign parents from document pages

1. **Navigate to the Pages panel** and locate the "Parents" section.

2. **Within the "Parents" section, select "None" as the parent.** This action will effectively unassign any existing parent from the chosen page.

When you remove a parent from a page, it results in the page's style and elements no longer inheriting characteristics from that parent. However, instead of completely unassigning the parent, you have the option to override specific parent items on individual document pages. This enables you to edit or modify these items exclusively on the chosen pages, providing flexibility when you need to retain most of the elements from a parent but wish to make specific alterations on certain pages. This approach allows for efficient customization without losing the overall structure provided by the parent.

Copy parent pages

1. **Copy from One Document to Another:**

   - Open the document where you want to establish a new parent.
   - Copy the desired parent from another document.
   - Paste the copied parent into the current document, creating a new parent relationship.

2. **Copy Within the Same Document:**

   - If you wish to duplicate a parent within the same document, copy the parent from its source.
   - Paste it onto another parent within the document, effectively creating a new parent based on the copied one.

3. **Copy to Other Documents:**

   - If you have a parent configured in one document and want to use it in others, copy the parent from the source document.
   - Paste the parent into the target document(s), establishing the same parent structure across multiple documents.

4. **Syncing Documents in a Book:**

   - If you are working with a book that contains multiple documents, sync the documents within the book.
   - This synchronization process can bring parent pages from one document into another, facilitating consistency across the entire book.

Copy a parent within a document

To replicate a parent spread within your document using the Pages panel, you can employ either of the following techniques:

1. **New Page Button:**

   - Within the Pages panel, locate and click on the "New Page" button positioned at the panel's bottom.
   - **Drag the page name of the desired parent spread to be duplicated and release it onto the newly generated page. This process effectively duplicates the parent spread.**

2. **Panel Menu Option:**

   - Identify the page name of the parent spread you intend to duplicate within the Pages panel.
   - **Right-click on the page name or access the panel menu.**
   - **From the available menu options, opt for "Duplicate Parent Spread [spread name]." This action duplicates the parent spread, generating a copy with an adjusted page prefix, typically advancing to the next letter in the alphabet.**

Upon copying a parent spread, it's important to note that the page prefix associated with the duplicated parent spread will automatically change to the next letter in the alphabet. These methods provide a straightforward way to replicate parent spreads, maintaining consistency and facilitating efficient page management within your document.

Copy or move a parent to another document

1. **Open Both Documents:**

   - Open the document where you intend to add the new parent.
   - Simultaneously, open the file that contains the parent you want to copy.

2. **Copy or Move Parent from Source Document:**

   - In the Pages panel of the source document:

     - To duplicate the entire parent spread, click and drag it to the window of the new document.
     - Alternatively, pick the specific parent you wish to copy or relocate.
     - Navigate to **"Layout > Pages > Move Parent"** in the menu.
     - From the "Move To" menu, designate the document name where you intend to relocate the parent.
     - If the intention is to eliminate the copied pages from the original file, opt for **"Delete Pages after Moving,"** and subsequently click OK.

3. **Address Duplicate Prefix:**

   - In cases where the target document already has a parent with the same prefix, the system automatically assigns the next letter in the alphabet to the moved parent. This ensures unique identification and avoids conflicts.

Delete a parent from a document

1. **Selecting Parent Page Icons:**

   - Head to the Pages panel.
   - **Choose one or more parent page icons slated for deletion.**
   - **Note: To obtain a list of all parent pages not currently in use, access the Page panel menu and opt for "Select Unused Parents."**

2. **Deletion Options:**

   - After selecting the parent page icons, proceed with one of the subsequent deletion methods:

     - Drag the chosen parent page or spread icon onto the "Delete" icon positioned at the base of the Pages panel.
     - Click the "Delete" button located at the panel's bottom.
     - Alternatively, access the panel menu, select **"Delete Parent Spread [spread name],"** and validate the deletion.

Upon deleting a parent, any page in the document associated with that parent will now have the [None] parent applied instead. This ensures that the document maintains a coherent structure even after the removal of a parent, with affected pages reverting to the default parent setting. These steps provide a straightforward way to manage and modify parent relationships within your document.

Override or detach parent items

When you introduce a parent page to a document page, all the elements present on the parent page, known as parent items, automatically appear on the document page. There are instances when you desire a document page to closely resemble a parent page. In such cases, you don't necessarily have to create a new parent or reconstruct the entire parent layout on the document page. Instead, you have the option to modify or eliminate specific parent items from the page, and the remaining parent elements will still update in tandem with the parent.

It's crucial to recognize that overriding parent items and removing them from a document page are distinct actions:

- **Overriding Parent Items:**

  - This involves modifying or altering specific parent items on a document page without completely removing them.
  - The overridden items on the document page will maintain their modified state independently of changes made to the parent.
  - This allows for customization on a per-page basis while retaining the overall structure from the parent.

- **Removing Parent Items from a Document Page:**

  - This action entails eliminating specific parent items from a document page entirely.

- Once removed, the document page will no longer display the removed parent items, and any updates to the parent will not affect these items on the document page.

Override parent item attributes

When a parent item is overridden on a document page, a duplicated version of the item is placed on the document page while maintaining a connection to the original parent page. This duplicated item, known as the local copy, allows for independent customization without affecting the parent. Following the override of an item, you gain the flexibility to selectively modify the attributes of the local copy to align with your preferences. For instance, you can adjust the fill color of the local copy, and any subsequent alterations to the fill color on the parent page will not affect the local copy. However, attributes such as size will consistently update according to changes made on the parent page unless specifically modified on the local copy. It's crucial to emphasize that the ability to revert to the parent's settings is retained by eliminating overrides. This procedural step ensures synchronization, ensuring that the object on the document page aligns with its parent.

Here are the characteristics you can modify for a parent page object on the document page:

- Strokes
- Fills
- Contents of a frame
- Transformations (rotating, scaling, shearing, resizing)
- Corner options
- Text frame options
- Lock state
- Transparency
- Object effects

Detach items from their parent

Indeed, the process of separating or detaching a parent item from its parent on a document page is possible. However, certain steps need to be followed:

1. **Override the Parent Item:**

    - Before detaching an item, it must be overridden on the document page, creating a local copy. This local copy becomes independent of the parent's changes.

2. **Detach the Item:**

    - Following the override, the item is eligible for detachment or separation from its association with the parent. This operation effectively severs the link between the local copy and the original parent page.

Post-detachment, the local copy of the item on the document page becomes isolated, ceasing to synchronize with any modifications made to the parent page. This independence facilitates distinctive customization, enabling unique adjustments without being influenced by changes applied to the parent.

Override a parent item

1. **Verify "Allow Parent Item Overrides":**

   - Confirm that the "Allow Parent Item Overrides On Selection" option is activated in the item's Pages panel menu. This setting dictates the permissibility of overriding the parent item.

2. **Override Specific Parent Items:**

   - **To override particular parent items on a document page:**

     - Hold down **Ctrl+Shift (Windows)** or **Command+Shift (Mac OS)**.
     - Click on the desired item to override (multiple items can be selected by dragging the cursor over them).
     - Modify the selected parent items to your preference. The overridden items can now be treated similarly to any other page items while maintaining linkage to the parent page.

3. **Override All Parent Page Items on a Spread:**

   - Alternatively, to override all parent page items on a spread:

     - Select a document spread.
     - From the Pages panel menu, opt for **"Override All Parent Page Items."**
     - Subsequently, each parent item on the spread can be independently modified.

The change in appearance, from a dotted box to a solid line around a parent item, signifies that a local copy has been generated.

Note: When replacing a linked text frame, all frames visible in that thread are also replaced, ensuring consistency in content across linked text frames even if they are on different pages in the spread.

Detach a parent item

1. **Override the Parent Item:**

   - Press **Ctrl+Shift (Windows)** or **Command+Shift (Mac OS)**.
   - Click on the specific item on the document page that you want to separate from its parent. This action overwrites the item, creating a local copy.

2. **Detach the Selection from Parent:**

   - After overriding the item, go to the Pages panel menu.
   - Select **"Detach Selection From Parent."**

This process disconnects the chosen parent item from its original parent, providing autonomy to the local copy. **If you want to remove all overridden parent items from a spread, use the following steps:**

1. **Select the Spread:**

   - In the document, choose the spread containing the overridden parent items.

2. **Remove Overridden Parent Page Items:**

   - Go to the Pages panel menu.
   - Select **"Detach All Objects From Parent."**

This action removes all overridden parent items on the selected spread. If the command is unavailable, it indicates that there are no modified items on that spread. These steps offer a precise way to manage the separation of individual parent items or remove all overridden parent items from a specific spread within your document.

Prevent a parent item from being overridden

When you need to override all parent items except a few on a document page, you can follow these steps:

1. **Select the Specific Parent Item:**

   - Pick out the parent item on the parent page that you want to keep unmodified.

2. **Disable Allow Parent Item Overrides On Selection:**

   - In the Pages panel menu, find the item you selected.
   - Uncheck the box that says **"Allow Parent Item Overrides on Selection."**

By unchecking this option, you prevent modifications to the selected parent item, ensuring it remains unchanged when overriding all other parent items on the document page. When parent items that don't allow modifications are displayed on the page, they have no frame edge, indicating that they are not open to overrides. If you decide to prevent a linked text frame from being overridden, the setting for all text frames in that thread remains consistent across the document.

Reapply parent items

If you inadvertently override parent elements, there's an option to revert them to their original state on the parent page. This action restores the object's properties to their parent-defined settings, ensuring subsequent updates when the parent is modified. The local copy of the object is removed, and the parent item becomes unselectable due to its bordered marking. You have the flexibility to eliminate modifications for specific objects or for all objects on a spread, although this operation can't be applied to the entire document simultaneously. This nuanced approach allows for targeted adjustments, ensuring precision in restoring or preserving modifications as needed.

1. **Eliminate Overrides on Selected Objects:**

- Choose the objects originally designated as parent items.
- **Select a spread in the Pages panel.**
- **Navigate to the Pages panel menu and opt for "Remove Selected Local Overrides."**
- **This action specifically eradicates overrides from the selected objects, allowing for the targeted reversal of particular modifications.**

2. **Remove All Overrides from a Spread:**

- Choose the spread (or parent spread) from which you intend to remove all parent overrides in the Pages panel.
- Ensure that no items are currently selected by going to **Edit > Deselect All.**
- From the Pages panel menu, choose **"Remove All Local Overrides."**

This command globally eliminates all parent overrides within the chosen spread, presenting a comprehensive solution for reverting modifications.

If objects are removed from a parent page, reintegrating them onto the parent page directly is not feasible. However, the option exists to delete the extracted objects and subsequently reinstate the parent onto the page. Upon restoring a parent to a page containing previously overridden parent page objects, the overridden items are expunged, and all parent page objects are reinstated. This process may result in some elements appearing duplicated on the page. To achieve an exact replication of the parent's appearance, it becomes imperative to eliminate the separately modified items.

Hide parent items

To conceal parent page items on specific pages in your document, you can utilize the Hide Parent Items tool with the following steps:

1. **Select Pages to Hide Parent Items:**

- In the Pages panel, identify and pick the spreads and pages where you wish to hide the parent items.

2. **Activate Hide Parent Items:**

- Access the Pages panel menu.
- Choose "Hide Parent Items" from the menu.

By following these steps, the parent items on the selected pages will be hidden, affecting the visual representation and print output of those items. This is useful when you want to temporarily remove certain elements from specific pages without permanently altering the document structure. **To reveal the hidden parent items again, use the following steps:**

1. **Select Spreads to Show Parent Items:**

- In the Pages panel, select the spreads containing the pages with hidden parent items.

2. **Reveal Hidden Parent Items:**

- Navigate to the Pages panel menu.
- Choose "Show Parent Items" from the menu.

These actions allow you to control the visibility of parent items on different pages, providing flexibility in managing the display and output of your document.

Import a parent from another document

1. **Open Load Parent Pages:**

   - Go to the Pages panel's menu.
   - Select "Load Parent Pages."

2. **Select Source InDesign File:**

   - Locate the InDesign file containing the parent pages you want to import.
   - Double-click on the file to initiate the import process.

3. **Handle Parent Name Conflicts:**

   - **Determine how conflicts with parent names should be resolved:**

     - **Replace Parent Pages:**

       - Choose this option if you want the parents from the source file to replace the parents with the same names in the target file.
       - Safe to use if the target document doesn't have any existing items with the same names as the incoming parents.

     - **Rename Parent Pages:**

       - Opt for this option to change the page names to start with the next letter in the alphabet, avoiding naming conflicts.

When working with parent pages in Adobe InDesign, it's crucial to understand the link established between the source document and the target document upon importing parent pages. **Here's a detailed explanation of how this process works:**

1. **Initial Import and Linking:**

   - Upon the transfer of parent pages from a source document to a target document, an intrinsic connection is established between the modified elements in the target document and their corresponding parent items on the freshly introduced parent pages.

This connection guarantees the synchronization of parent pages across different documents, negating the necessity to consolidate these documents into a book.

2. **Ensuring Consistency:**

   - To uphold consistency among parent pages across diverse documents, it is advisable to load the parent pages from the source document before initiating any modifications to objects on the parent pages in the target document.

3. **Management of Overridden Elements:**

   - In instances where overridden items exist in the document (i.e., alterations made to items on the parent pages) without the import of their parents from another source, these overridden items undergo segregation upon the initial loading of parent pages from a source document.

4. **Replacement of Parent Pages:**

   - When introducing parents from a different source document and opting for the replacement of parent pages, the items that underwent modifications in the target document may undergo separation.

   - **Any parent pages with matching names in the new source document will be applied to the pages of the target document that contain altered items. This scenario may result in the presence of two sets of objects if not handled with due care.**

It's crucial to plan and sequence your actions when working with parent pages, especially when importing them from different source documents. By understanding the link and considering the order of operations, you can effectively maintain consistency and avoid unintended consequences in your InDesign projects.

CHAPTER 5: MASTERING TEXT TOOLS

ADDING AND FORMATTING TEXT

It's time to add information to your document after you've set up its simple layout. Since text is a big part of most InDesign jobs, this is the best place to begin.

There are text boxes in an InDesign document that hold all of the text. You can have as many text boxes of any shape and size as you want. The text boxes can also be linked to each other so that long stretches of text that don't fit in one box will flow into the next linked text box. You can use the Tools panel or the keyboard shortcut T to switch to the Text tool. To make a text box, click and drag on a blank page. You can now put in the text you want to typeset or use Adobe's famous Lorem Ipsum blank text to fill in the text box. This feature is so useful that Adobe made it a built-in feature.

As soon as you click on a text box, the Control panel at the top of InDesign will show you different ways to style the text. You can pick the font you want to use and change its size, heading, and other stylistic settings. You can use these settings on whole text boxes or just the part of the text you've chosen, but there's a better way. Instead of formatting each part of your text separately, it's better to use paragraph styles to tag each piece of your text. These styles can then be used again and again. This way, all of your headlines will be formatted in a new way.

When you open InDesign or any other Creative Cloud app from Adobe, a basic set of fonts is already there. However, if you want some new font ideas, you can easily add new fonts. As part of your Creative Cloud account, you can look through the online collection of Adobe Fonts. With just a few clicks, a new font will be linked and ready to use in InDesign.

CREATE TEXT FRAMES

In InDesign, text lives in boxes called "text frames." (In QuarkXPress and Adobe PageMaker, a text frame is like a text box and a text block.) Frame grids and plain text frames are the two kinds of text frames. Frame grids are the type of text frames that are only used for writing in Asian languages. They show character emboxes and space as grids. Texts frames that are empty and don't have a grid are called "plain text frames."

Word and text frames can be moved, resized, and changed, just like graphic frames. What changes you can make depend on the tool you use to choose a text frame:

- To add or edit text in a frame, use the Type tool T.

- Use the Selection tool to do general layout work, like putting a frame in the right place and making it the right size.

- To change the shape of a frame, use the Direct Selection tool.

- To make a frame grid, use either the Horizontal Grid tool or the Vertical Grid tool.

- To make a plain text frame for horizontal text, use the Type tool T. To make a plain text frame for vertical text, use the Vertical Type tool ↓T. You can change text that is already in a frame with the same tools.

It is also possible to link text frames together so that the text in one frame can move to another frame. When frames are linked in this way, they are called "threaded." A story is a piece of writing that moves through one or more threaded frames. No matter how many frames a word processing file takes up, when you place (import) it, it comes into your document as a single story. Text frames can have more than one column. While text frames can be built on page columns, they can also work without them. That is, a text frame with two columns can fit on a page with four columns. Text frames can be put on parent pages as well, and they can still get text from document pages. **Note: If you use the same kind of text frame over and over, you can make an object style that has choices for text frames, stroke and fill colors, text wrap and transparency effects, and text frame styling. InDesign adds text frames instantly based on the page's column settings, so you don't have to make them before you place or put text. A plain text box is made naturally when text is added. You can also manually make a plain text frame that is empty and then type text into it.**

1. **Do any of these things:**

   - Choose the Type tool T and then drag to set the new text frame's width and height. To make the frame into a square, hold down Shift and drag. When you let go of the mouse button, a text entry point shows up on the screen.

Dragging to create new text frame

Click the in or out port of another text frame with the Selection tool, and then click or drag to make a new frame.

To put a text file somewhere, use the Place command.

Click inside any empty frame with the Type tool T. The empty frame is turned into a text frame if the Type Tool Converts Frames To Text Frames option is chosen in the Type preferences.

Move and resize text frames

You can move or change the size of text frames with the Selection tool. **Note: If you want to move or change the size of a text frame without moving from the Type tool** T **to a selection tool, hold down Ctrl (Windows) or Command (Mac OS) and drag the frame.**

Move a text frame

- Drag the frame with the Selection tool.

- Hold down Ctrl (Windows) or Command (Mac OS) and drag the frame with the Type tool. The Type tool is still chosen when you let go of the key.

Resize a text frame

1. **Do any of these things:**

   - Hold down Ctrl (Windows) or Command (Mac OS) and drag any frame handle to change the size of the Type tool T. The text will be put back together while you change the size of the frame if you hold down the mouse button for one second before you start to drag.

Note: If you click on the text frame instead of dragging it, you will lose where you had the text selected or where you had the entry point.

- To change the size of a frame with the Selection tool ➤, drag any of the frame handles on the edge of the frame. To change the size of the words in the frame, hold down Ctrl (Windows) or Command (Mac OS).

- To quickly make the frame fit the text inside it, pick the text frame with the Selection tool and double-click any handle. This will make the bottom of the frame snap to the bottom of the text: double-click the center bottom handle. If you double-click the handle in the middle-right corner, the height stays the same but the width gets smaller to fit the frame.

TIP: You can also double-click on a handle on an overset text frame to make the frame wider or taller so that all the text fits inside. If there is more overset text in a text frame than can fit on the page, the text frame is not expanded.

- To make the text frame fit the content, use the Selection tool to pick the frame and then go to **Object > Fitting > Fit Frame to Content**. The bottom of the text frame is big enough for the text. If there is more overset text in a text frame than can fit on the page, the text frame is not expanded.

- Drag the frame to change its size with the Scale tool.

Use text frames on parent pages

As soon as you start a new document, you can choose the Primary Text Frame option to put an empty text frame on the document's default parent page. In the New Document window box, the column and border settings were set for this frame.

If you want to use text frames on parent pages, follow these rules:

- Use primary text frames when you want a page-sized text frame on every page of your document. You can flow or type your text into these frames. Leave the Primary Text Frame option unchecked and use the Type tool to add text frames to parents if your document needs more variety, like pages with different amounts of frames or frames of different lengths.

- You can add text frames to a parent page to use as placeholders even if you don't choose the Primary Text Frame choice. These empty frames can be put next to each other to make a flow.

- Use the same steps you would use for frames made on document pages to flow text into primary text frames.

- To type text in a document page's primary text frame, hold down Ctrl+Shift (Windows) or Command+Shift (Mac OS) and click on the frame. Then, use the Type tool to click in the frame and start typing.

- Smart Text Reflow can bring in or take out pages automatically as you type or change text. When you type at the end of a linked text frame that is based on a parent page, a new page is added so that you can keep typing in the new text frame. You can change the settings for Smart Text Reflow.

- If you change the page margins, text frames will only change to fit the new margins if the "Enable Layout Adjustment" option is checked.

- If you choose the Primary Text Frame choice, new pages will be added when you autoflow text.

PARAGRAPH AND CHARACTER STYLES

Open the Paragraph Styles window first. Press F11 or go to Window > Styles > Paragraph Styles if it's not already open. You might find that this opens the Character Styles box too. Okay, you'll need it too.

In InDesign, you can put the window anywhere you want. It can be docked on the left or right, but for now, we're going to leave it floating.

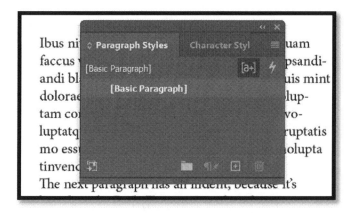

There will already be the [Basic Paragraph] style on your page. Until you choose another style, this is the one that will be used in the new text. You can change this, but not delete it or give it a new name. It will open the Paragraph Styles Options box if you double-click on it.

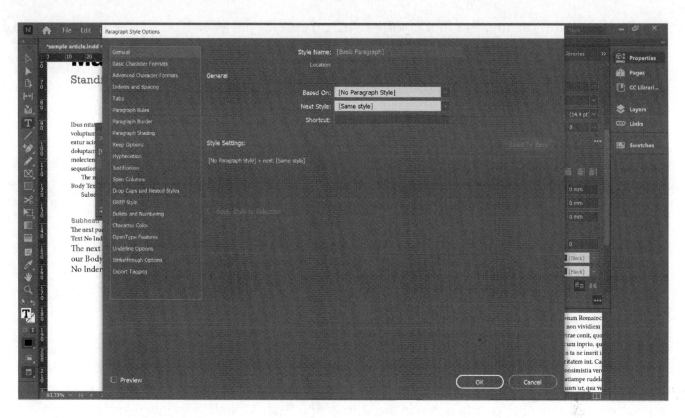

You can see here how many formatting options are saved in a paragraph style. You can create styles this way, but it's faster to base forms on words that you already have.

First, let's look at a simple two-page document with two headlines, two standfirsts, five subheadings, and some blank text in between the parts. Everything is in the [Basic Paragraph] style at this point.

You can make your first headline look however you want. We picked Arial Black at 30pt for this project. For some reason, the font color is black. You can put your type tool anywhere in the headline text. Click the plus sign at the bottom of the Paragraph Styles box. This will make Paragraph Style 1. If you want to, you can also use the InDesign Story Editor to pick text and change it.

You should name this something more interesting. Left-click the paragraph style name for about half a second and left-click again. You should now be able to change the name of the paragraph style. You can also change the name in the Paragraph Style Options window, which you can get to by clicking on the name of the paragraph style twice.

Because we're going to use it for headlines, we named our new paragraph style Headlines. Now, go to the second page and find Main Headline Number 2. Place the mouse anywhere in the headline and choose the Headlines paragraph style that you just set up.

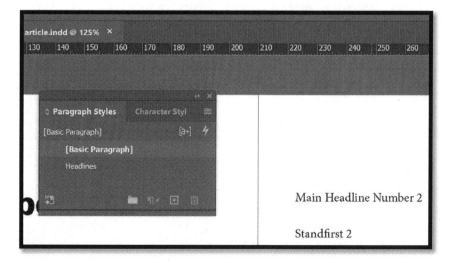

Right now, this headline looks just like the first one.

For your standfirsts, follow the same steps, but this time try adding a different color. We chose the color red. This data will be saved by InDesign in both the word and paragraph styles.

Now let's talk about the subheads. We're going to change not only the font and color this time but also the space between the letters (tracking). We'll also make the lines more spaced out (leading), so there will always be a space above the subheads. We have Arial Bold set to 12pt with 23pt Leading and Tracking set to 20 as shown in the picture below. It is also set to blue.

This style can now be used in the rest of your document. You can see how this can save you time when you need to prepare parts of your document that are the same.

NESTED STYLES AND ADVANCED TYPOGRAPHIC SETTINGS

For one or more groups of characters inside a line or paragraph, you can give them different styles. You can even set up two or more stacked styles to work together, with each style picking up where the one before it left off. There is also the option of going back to the first style in the list for paragraphs with layout that is the same and easy to spot. To make run-in headlines look better, nested styles are very useful. For instance, you can use one character style on the first letter of a paragraph and then use a different style that runs through the first colon (:). For each stacked style, you can say which character ends the style. This character could be the end of a word or a tab character.

Create one or more nested styles

What to do:

1. One thing you need to do before you can format text is make one or more character styles.

2. **Choose one of the options below:**

    - To add nested styles to a paragraph style, double-click the paragraph style and then click the Drop Caps and Nested Styles button.

    - Take a look at the choices in the Paragraph box and choose Drop Caps and Nested Styles. This will add nested styles to a single paragraph.

The best results will be achieved by using nested styles as part of paragraph styles. If you apply nested styles to a paragraph as local overrides, changing or formatting changes in the nested style in the future could cause character formatting changes in the styled text that you didn't expect. This could lead to characters being formatted in a way that isn't expected.

3. Choose "New Nested Style" and tap it at least once.

4. Pick one of these choices for each style, then click the OK button:

- You can change the way that part of the paragraph looks by clicking on the character style area and then choosing a style from the list that comes up. If you don't already have a character style, select "New Character Style" and then describe the formatting you want to use.

- Please choose the item that ends the formatting of the character style. On top of that, you can type the character, which could be a colon (;) or a specific letter or number.

- Give the number of times the chosen item has to be used, like the number of lines, words, or sentences that are needed.

- From the menu, choose either through or Up To. When you choose through, the formatting includes the character that finishes the nested style. But when you choose Up To, the formatting only includes the characters that come before this character.

- Choose a style and then click either the up▲ or down▼ button to change the order of the styles in the list. The order in which the styles are applied determines the order in which the coding is applied. When the formatting for the first style ends, the formatting for the second style begins. There is an order of styles, and the drop-cap character style is the first one that will work if a style is given to it.

Loop through nested styles

You can use a series of two or more nested styles in the same paragraph at the same time. One simple way to show this is to change the words in a paragraph from red to green. You could also use nested line styles to make a paragraph with red and green lines that go back and forth. The repeated pattern will stay the same no matter how many words you add or take away from the paragraph.

These are the steps:

1. Generate the character types you want to use.

2. Either change a current paragraph style or make a new one. You can also paste the entry point into the paragraph and format it.

3. Choose **New Nested Style** (or **New Nested Line Style**) at least twice in the area or dialog box called Drop Caps and Nested Styles. Then, choose the settings you want for each style.

4. **Do any of these things:**

- In the character style box, select **[Repeat]**. Then, click **New Nested Style** a second time to use nested styles. Lastly, you need to set how many nested styles will be used again.

- After clicking **New Nested Line Style** a second time, you will need to set the number of lines that will be repeated and then choose **[Repeat]** from the character style menu.

There are times when you can skip the first style or styles. **"This Week's Events"** might be the first sentence of a paragraph on an events calendar, and then the activities planned for each day of the week would follow. The first nested style would be left out of the loop if you created five nested styles in this case: one for **"This Week's Events,"** one for the day, one for the event, one for the event time, and a final style with a [Repeat] number of three. **"Repeat"** should be the last thing on the list. Any style that is placed below the [Repeat] element is not taken into account.

5. Click the "**OK**" button.

TEXT IMPORT AND EXPORT

Adding text from different sources to Adobe InDesign is something you will probably have to do a lot when working on print and web design projects. That's possible with InDesign because it works with many file types. You can then add text from many sources.

Here's how to bring in text from different places:

1. Open Adobe InDesign to begin.
2. You need to either start a new project or open an old one to add text to an existing InDesign document.
3. Before you add text, you need to make a text frame. To do this, select the "**Type Tool**" from the menu and click and drag on the page to choose where you want the text to go.
4. You can achieve this by pressing Ctrl + D (Windows) or Cmd + D (Mac), or you can go to **File > Place**.

5. Find the saved plain text file (TXT) and click on it.
6. Pick "**Open**."
7. Choose the same thing, which is **File > Place**.

8. Look for the document that Microsoft Word generated and click on it. After that, click "Open."
9. If you want to add RTF files along with plain text, you need to follow the steps for adding plain text.
10. InDesign can also bring text straight from PDF files. Select Place from the File menu to pick out the PDF file.
11. Choose the PDF page or pages that you want to use. After that, click Open.
12. When you add text, you can either link it to it or make it part of your document. If you use linked text, any changes you make to the outside file will show up in InDesign. Once the text is integrated, it becomes part of the InDesign document and doesn't need to be linked to a source file.
13. Another box called "Text Import Options" might show up after you choose a file. This will let you choose settings like styles, formatting, and more.
14. You can group text frames together if the received text is longer than the first text frame. First, click on the result of the first text frame. Then, click right on top of the second text frame.
15. Check to make sure that the imported formatting, fonts, and special characters are used correctly. If needed, formatting and styles should be changed.
16. If you have linked text, keep track of the files that are linked. If the source files have been changed, you can change the links in InDesign.
17. Once the text is in the document, you should make any last changes you need to the layout, formatting, and styles.
18. To keep all of the changes and import settings, you must remember to save your InDesign document.
19. You can either share or print the document when you're done with your creation.

EXPORTING TEXT FOR COLLABORATION AND OTHER APPLICATIONS

These are the steps:

1. Open Adobe InDesign first, then the document containing the words you want to export.

2. **Make sure your document's settings are right before you export it. Look at the following things:**

    - **Fonts:** Make sure that the fonts you've chosen can be found on other websites or are embedded on your own. You can add fonts to the document package by going to **"File"** > **"Package"** and then following the on-screen steps. This will let you add fonts.

    - **Images:** When you add pictures to a document, you need to make sure they properly connect. Click **"Window"** and then **"Links"** to see and change photos that are linked.

3. The Text tool can help you choose the text that you want to send. To pick all the words in the document, you can also press the Ctrl+A (Windows) or Command+A (Mac) keys at the same time.

4. After selecting the text, you can copy it to the clipboard by holding down the Ctrl and C keys (Windows) or the Command and C keys (Mac).

5. Open a text editor (like Notepad on Windows or TextEdit on Mac) and press Ctrl+V (Windows) or Command+V (Mac) at the same time to paste the text you copied. Make sure the file ends in .txt when you save it.

6. Should you wish to keep some of the formatting, you can save the text in Rich Text Format (RTF). Start up a text editor, copy and paste the text, and then save the file with the .rtf name.

7. If you want to easily export the whole document while keeping the layout, you should save it as a PDF. Simply go to the **"File"** menu, pick **"Export,"** pick **"PDF"** as the format, make any necessary changes, and then hit **"Export."**

8. To make it easier for people to work together on the project, export the whole InDesign document as an InDesign Markup Language (IDML) file. Go to the **"File"** menu, pick **"Export,"** and choose "InDesign Markup (IDML)" as the default format. Then hit **"Save."**

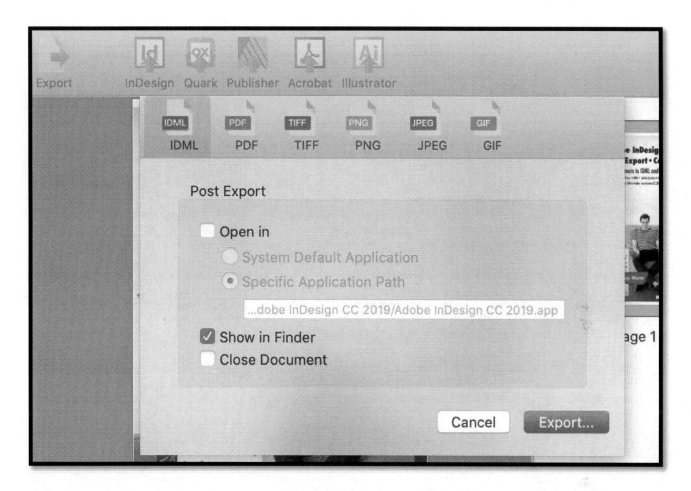

9. Email the exported file to other people, store it in the cloud, or use any other tool that makes working together easier. Make sure the readers have access to the necessary fonts and files if you plan to share the InDesign document with them.

Export each story in a different text file (script included in InDesign)

The Adobe team added some tools that you can use to make simple tasks run automatically. There are apps to show you what you can do with a little code in InDesign. There is a script in this group called "Exportallstories" that does exactly what its name says. Double-clicking on "Exportallstories" makes a copy of the text in each story of your document in a text file.

Here's what you need to do to run the script:

1. Click on **Window** > **Utilities** > **Scripts** to open the Scripts Panel.

2. Go to the folder **Application** > **Samples** > **JavaScript** in the **Scripts Panel**.

3. Select the appropriate file and set the location by double-clicking Exportallstories.jsx.

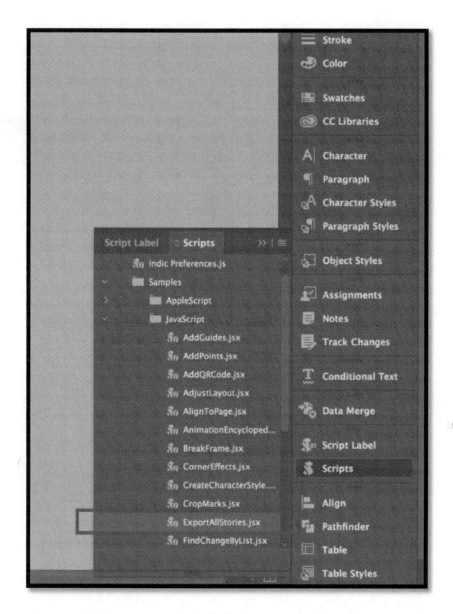

As we already said, the script will make a document for each story in your InDesign file. You should try out all the text formats and then choose the one that works best for you. Since you can export the formatting with RTF, I think your choice will be between Text Only and RTF.

CHAPTER 6: LEVERAGING OBJECT STYLES

Similar to how paragraph and character styles make formatting text easier, Adobe InDesign's object styles make formatting images and frames quick and easy. There are a lot of different choices in these styles, like stroke, color, transparency, drop shadows, paragraph styles, text wrap, and more. An extensive toolset for design customization is provided by the transparency effects that can be applied to the object, fill, line, and text. Object styles can be used on many things, like objects, groups, frames, and even text frames. Styles can change all of an object's settings at once or just some of them while leaving others alone. This is possible by changing the values in the style description, which lets users pick which settings the style affects. If you work with frame grids, object styles make it easy to change how they look.

Any new frame grid starts out with the [Basic Grid] object style, but users can change this style or add more object styles to improve the grid's look. Users can choose factors like writing direction, frame type, and the called grid in the Story Options area when making or changing an object style for a frame grid. Users will notice that many styles have characteristics that are the same, which makes the process of making styles faster. Instead of constantly describing these traits, a new object style can be based on an existing character style. Using this method makes it easier to make new styles because when changes are made to the base style, all shared traits in the "parent" style are instantly updated in the "child" style that goes with it. This layered arrangement of styles helps keep things consistent and speeds up the planning process.

DEFINING AND APPLYING OBJECT STYLES FOR CONSISTENT DESIGN

In just three steps, you can make an InDesign object style. You'll be able to get more done faster because object styles will make your work easier. You know that paragraph styles and character styles work great, right? Actually, object styles work the same way. Book Design Made Simple (see below) has steps on how to set up object styles in InDesign. After creating the object styles in InDesign, using them is the same as using paragraph or character styles. You need to choose a shape, line, text frame, or picture frame that is already set up the way you want it to be before you can make an object style.

Simply follow these steps:

1. Click Window, then Styles, then Object Styles to open the Object Styles panel.

2. Choose a shape, line, or frame with the Selection Tool.

3. Select New Object Style from the drop-down menu in the Object Styles window. Type what's shown below into the box, and then click OK.

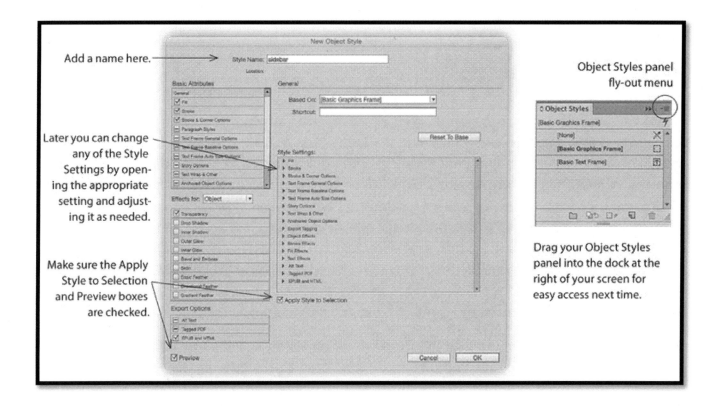

Add a name here.

Later you can change any of the Style Settings by opening the appropriate setting and adjusting it as needed.

Make sure the Apply Style to Selection and Preview boxes are checked.

Object Styles panel fly-out menu

Drag your Object Styles panel into the dock at the right of your screen for easy access next time.

UPDATING STYLES FOR SEAMLESS WORKFLOW

It's easy to keep things consistent and make work move more smoothly when you update styles in Adobe InDesign. There are many types of styles in InDesign, such as character styles, object styles, paragraph styles, and more.

Here is a guide on how to properly change styles:

1. **Open the Styles Panel:** Start by opening the Styles Panel. To do this, go to the "Window" menu and choose "Styles."

2. **Select the Style to Update:** From the Styles panel, pick out the style type you want to update (paragraph, character, etc.).

3. **Update Paragraph Styles:**

   - If you're changing the style of a paragraph, change the layout of the chosen text to match the new style (font, size, spacing, etc.).

   - To change the style, right-click on it in the Styles panel and pick "Redefine Style."

4. **Update Character Styles:**

   - Choose the text that has the character style you want to update, just like you did with paragraph styles.

   - Make changes to the text's size, color, font, etc.

   - To update the style, right-click on it in the Styles box and pick "Redefine Style."

5. **Update Object Styles:**

   - If you are working with objects, pick out one that has the style you want to update.

   - Make the changes that need to be made, like stroke, fill, effects, and so on.

   - To change the style, right-click on it in the Styles box and pick "Redefine Style."

6. **Based On:** When making or updating styles, use the "Based On" function. By connecting a new style to an old one, this makes it easier to stay consistent.

7. **Load Styles:** Using the "Load Styles" option in the Styles panel menu, you can import styles from another document or template into your current document.

8. **Update All Instances:** If you update a style, InDesign may ask you if you want to change all cases of that style in the document. Click "Update All" to get a full fix.

9. **Use Object Styles for Consistent Graphic Elements:** Make and use Object Styles for frames, pictures, shapes, and other graphic elements. This keeps the look and style consistent.

10. **Preview Changes:** In the Styles panel, turn on "Preview" to see the changes as they happen in real-time before applying them.

11. **Document-wide Changes:** If you need to make changes that affect many documents at once, use the "Load All Text and Objects" option in the Styles panel menu.

12. **Keep a Style Guide:** To make sure everything is the same, make a style guide for your document. You can put information in this book about fonts, colors, space, and how to use different styles.

Updating styles in InDesign can make your work much easier and make sure that your document looks professional and organized. Reviewing and improving your styles on a regular basis helps keep things consistent and makes it easier to adapt to changes in your design.

CHAPTER 7: ENHANCING TEXT LAYOUT

TEXT WRAPPING AND ANCHORED OBJECTS

Activating the Text Wrap Panel

The Text Wrap panel lets you change how each object is wrapped. You can also find the same choices in the menu bar.

1. The panel will appear when you click on **Window** and then **Text Wrap**.

Wrap the text

Once you put an object in InDesign, it is set to **No Text Wrap (A)**.

To change this choice, click on the object. You can alter it to:

- **B. Wrap around Bounding Box:** makes the text go all the way around the bounding box.

- **C. Wrap around Object Shape:** This option makes a text-wrap border around the shape you chose. This choice is cool because it can also find the edges of a picture and wrap the text around them.

- **D. Jump Object:** When you use Jump Object, the text will be forced to appear above and below the object. It will not appear next to the object at all.

- **E. Jump To Next Column:** When you click on "Jump To Next Column," the paragraph around it moves to the top of the next column/text frame.

For each choice, this is what happened:

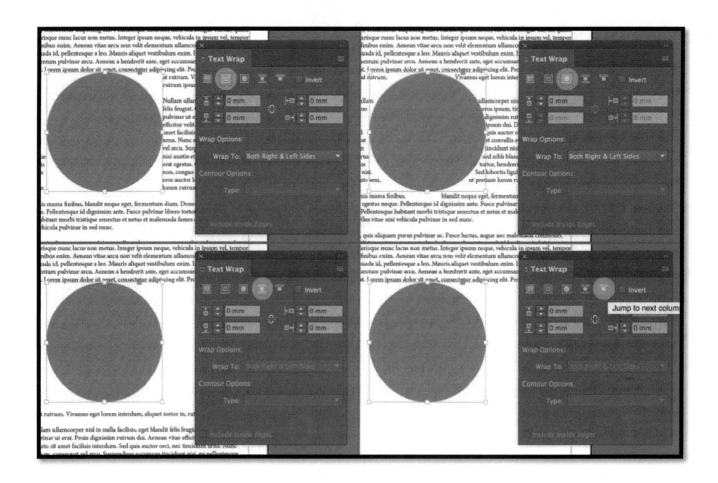

Adjust the distance between text and object

By changing the offset numbers and the wrap choices, you can change the space between the text and the edges of the object.

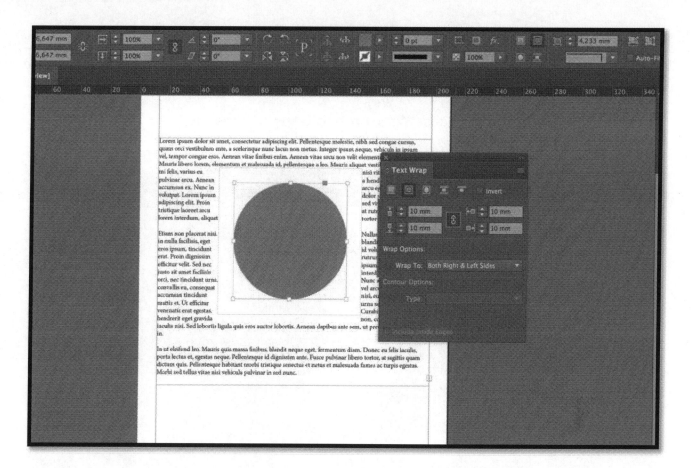

You can later change this boundary by using the Direct Selection tool (the white arrow to be clearer) or the Pen tool.

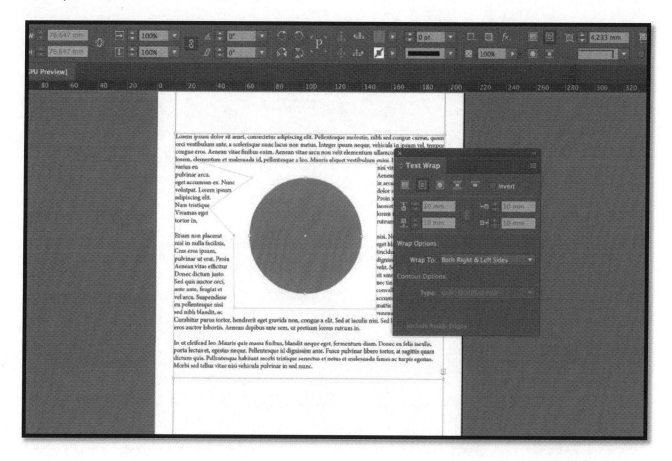

Detect the edges of an image when text wrapping

When InDesign finds the edge of a picture, it makes a boundary that you can use to wrap text around it (or inside the picture).

1. In the Text Wrap Panel, choose **Wrap around Object Shape**. Next, set the type to **Detect Edges**.

2. You can change how the edges are found by picking the object and going to **Object > Clipping Path > Options**.

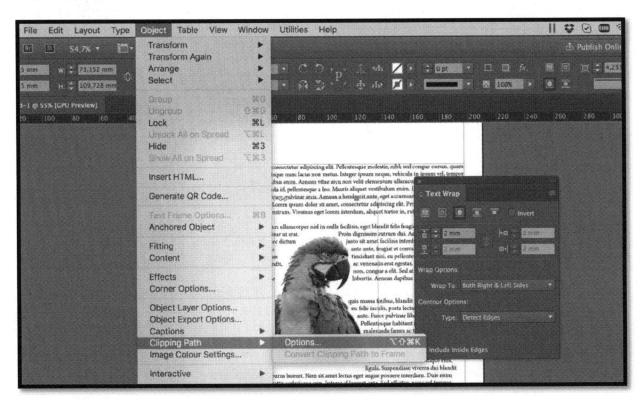

WRAP TEXT AROUND IMAGES WITH CAPTION

As a whole, a group of objects works like a single object. Putting an image and a description into a group and then setting Text Wrap to the group is the best way to wrap the text around the image and caption.

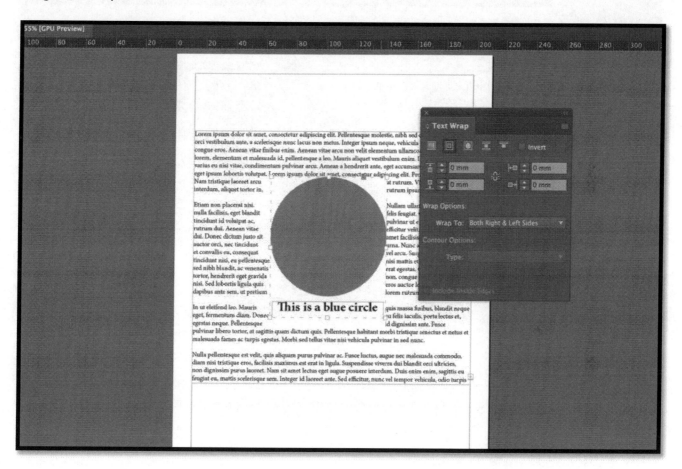

Wrap text around an anchored object or an inline object

The text wrap character properties of an anchored object only affect the lines of text that come after the anchor marker; the lines of text that come before the anchor marker and the line in which the anchor marker is placed are unaffected by these characteristics. Inline things are also anchored objects, so the same rule applies to them as well.

Text wraps and master pages

You can choose to have the text always wrap around the picture around objects that are put into master pages (this is the usual setting when Text Wrap is turned on), or you can turn on the Apply to Master Page Only option to only apply the text that is put into the master page.

Text wrap and hidden layers

If you don't hide the layer that a wrap object is connected to, it will still affect text frames in all of them. The choice to "Suppress Text Wrap When Layer Is Hidden" will be available in the Layer Options dialog box. When you choose this option, the behavior can be changed. The text that is placed on other levels can be rearranged as a result of this choice.

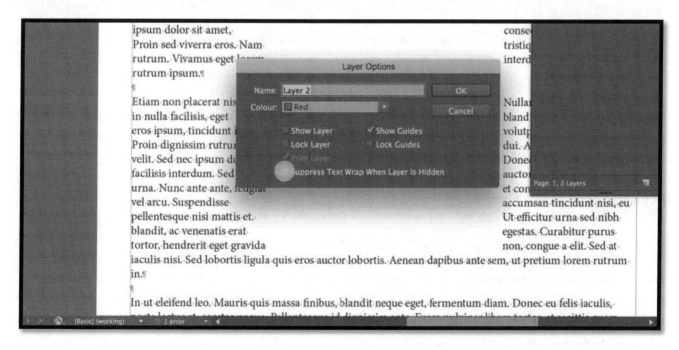

Create an anchored object

If an object isn't ready to be put on the page, you can make an empty anchored frame to hold information that you will be able to add later. For example, section text that hasn't been written yet. You can change the size of the connected frame at any time, and the position settings for the frame will change right away.

1. **First, do any of the following:**

    - To add an object that is anchored; first use the Type tool to set an entry point where you want the object's anchor to show up. Then, either drag and drop the object into place or paste it there.

Text can go beyond the downloaded picture, or you may see extra space above the line if the object's frame is longer than the text line it's in. If this is the case, the picture you imported won't show up. You may be able to change the size of the inline object, choose a different anchored object location, add a soft or hard line break, or change the leading value for the lines that surround it.

- To anchor an object, first choose it and then go to **Edit > Cut** from the menu that comes up. The next step is to set the entry point with the Type tool where you want the object to show itself, then select **Edit > Paste** from the menu. The location of the attached object is inline in the default setting.

- If you want to make a placeholder frame for an object that isn't available yet, like text you haven't written for a sidebar, use the Type tool to find the point where you want the object's link to show up. Then, from the menu that comes up, choose **Object > Anchored Object > Insert**.

Before you can connect text characters, you need to make sketches of the text around them. Each character of text is instantly turned into an inline fixed object when outlines are made.

2. Pick out the object you want to place with a selection tool. Then, from the menu that comes up, choose **Object > Anchored Object > Options**. You can choose which choices you want.

You might not have to go through the Anchored Object dialog box first if you use the computer function for Insert Anchored Object/Go to Anchor Marker. In the Text and Tables area, you can find the Keyboard Tool Editor. You will need to give shortcut keys to this tool there. If you press the shortcut twice, the object is removed from the selection, and the mouse is returned to the main text.

CREATING AND FORMATTING TABLES

Rows and columns are used to arrange the cells that make up a table. You can add text, inline graphics, and other tables to a cell, which works a lot like a text frame with the same name. Making a table can be done from scratch or by changing text that already appears in a table. You can also add a table inside of another table. The width of the container text frame is filled by the new table that you make after making the first table. A table is put on the same line as the placement point, which is at the beginning of the line. If you put the entry point in the middle of a line, a table will be written on the line that comes after it. Tables work the same way that inline graphics do: they blend in with the text around them. When the point size of the text above the table changes or when content is added or removed, for example, the table will move between linked frames. It is not possible for a table to be on a text-on-path frame, though. When you use InDesign to make a table, you can also put the table inside a text frame that is already there. If you want, you can also tell InDesign to make the text frame that goes around the table you've made.

Using the Insert Table Option

1. Use the Type tool to create a table inside a text frame that is already there. Then, place the insertion point where you want the table to show up while you are drawing.

2. Go to the menu and choose **Table > Insert Table**.

The "Create Table" choice can be chosen if the mouse is not in a text frame at the moment.

3. Say how many rows and columns are in the table as a whole.

4. If the information in your table will go across more than one column or frame, you will need to say the number of header or footer rows you want the information to appear again.

5. Pick a table style (you don't have to do this step).

6. Click the "**OK**" button. The new table will take up the whole width of the text frame.

Using the Create Table Option

When you will be using the Create Table option to make a table, it is not necessary to first create a text frame in your document. When you're done drawing the table on the page, InDesign will make a text frame that is the same size as the table right away.

1. Go to the menu and choose **Table > Create Table**.

Additionally, the Insert Table option can be used if the mouse is currently in a text frame.

2. Say how many rows and columns are in the table as a whole.

3. If the information in your table will go across more than one column or frame, you will need to say the number of header or footer rows you want the information to appear again.

4. Pick the table style you want.

5. Click the "OK" button.

6. You need to use the Table cursor to create the table you want.

The table is put inside the text frame that InDesign makes, which is the same size as the area that was drawn. For each table, the row height will depend on the table style that is chosen. For example, cell styles can be used in a table style to arrange different parts of the table. If any of these cell styles have paragraph styles in them, the leading number of the paragraph styles determines the row height of that area. As long as there are no paragraph styles on the page, the document's default slug sets the row height. The starting number determines the slug. In this case, the slug is the height of the underlined text in the picked text.

Create a table from existing text

It is important to make sure that the text is formatted properly before turning it into a table.

1. Separate the text into columns by adding tabs, commas, paragraph returns, or any other character. This will get it ready for change. You can use any character, like tabs, commas, paragraph returns, or anything else, to tell rows apart. "There are many times when text can be turned into a table without any changes needing to be made."

2. Figure out the text you want to turn into a table by selecting it with the Type tool.

3. From the menu, choose Table > Convert Text to Table.

4. For both the Column Separator and the Row Separator, you need to mark the start of new rows and columns. There are three options for the column and row separators: Tab, Comma, and Paragraph. You can also type a character, like the semicolon (;), to use as a divider. Any character you type will show up in the menu with the table the next time you make one from text.

5. You will need to tell the script how many columns you want the table to have if you want to use the same divider between rows and columns.

6. If you want, you can format the table by choosing a table style.

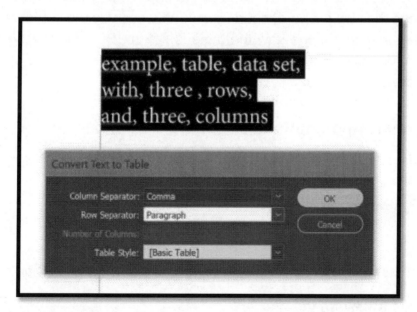

Example: table, data set, with, three, rows, and, three, columns

7. Click the "OK" button.

If any rows don't have enough things for the number of columns in the table, the empty cells are filled in.

Insert/embed a table inside of another table

What to do:

1. **First, do any of the following:**

   - Pick out the cells or table you want to embed. Go to **Edit > Cut or Copy** from the menu that comes up. Place the entry point in the cell where you want the table to show up. Next, go to the menu bar and select **Edit > Paste**.

   - When you click inside a cell, a menu pops up. Choose **Table > Insert Table** from that menu. Then, set the number of rows and columns, and finally click OK.

2. Make any changes to the cell inset that are needed.

You will not be able to use the mouse to select any part of the table that goes beyond the edge of the cell if you make it inside a cell. To fix this, you should either make the row or column bigger, or you could put the entry point at the beginning of the table and use the keyboard to move it and pick text for the table.

FORMATTING TABLES

The Control panel or Character panel can be used to style text inside a table in the same way it can be used for text outside of a table. There are two main window boxes that help you arrange the table: Table Options and Cell Options. With these window boxes, you can change the number of rows and columns, add more table formatting, change the space above and below the table, and change the way the border and fill look. You can use the context menu, the Control panel, or the Table panel to change how the table is set up. By right-clicking (on Windows) or Control-clicking (on Mac OS), you can bring up a context menu with table options after you've selected one or more cells.

Adjust tables, rows, and columns

You can change the size of columns, rows, and tables in a lot of different ways.

Resize columns and rows

How to do it:

1. Pick out the cells from the columns and rows that you want to change the size of.

2. **Do any of the following things:**

   - In the Table panel, set the Column Width and Row Height settings.

- Choose **Table > Cell Options > Rows and Columns**. Then, enter the values you want for Column Width and Row Height. Finally, click OK to finish.

If you choose the "At Least" option for a minimum row height, rows will get taller when you add text or make the points bigger. It doesn't matter if you add or remove text when you choose exactly for a fixed row height. There is often an overset situation in the cell when the row height is fixed.

- The double-arrow icon will show up when you move the pointer over the edge of a row or column. Then, drag the sliders up or down to change the height of the row or left or right to change the width of the column.

Row height is set by the slug height of the current font. So, changing the row height setting or the point size of the font across a row of text also changes the row height. The maximum row height is set by the Maximum option in the Rows and Columns section of the Cell Options dialog box.

Adjust columns or rows without affecting the table width

You can change the number of columns or rows without changing the width of the table. To do this:

- Hold down Shift and drag an inner row or column edge (not the table border). As one row or column gets smaller, the other ones get bigger.

- To make rows or columns fit better, hold down Shift and drag the bottom or right edges of the table.

Hold down Shift and drag the right table edge to change the sizes of all the columns. Hold down Shift and drag the bottom table edge to change the sizes of all the rows.

Resize the entire table

The steps:

1. Use the Type tool to move the pointer to the bottom right corner of the table until it turns into an arrow shape. This will change the size of the table. For the table's height and width to stay the same, hold down Shift.

Note: If the table in a story spans more than one frame, you can't use the pointer to make the whole table bigger.

Distribute columns and rows evenly

1. Pick the cells in rows or columns that are the same width or height.

2. Go to Table and choose either Distribute Columns Evenly or Distribute Rows Evenly.

Adjust the distance before and after a table

1. Once the insertion point is in the table, go to Table > Table Options > Table Setup.

2. Different values should be chosen for Space Before and Space After under Table Spacing. Then click OK to finish.

When the space before the table is changed, the space between the rows of a table that ends at the top of a frame stays the same.

Add text to a table

People can add things like text, anchored objects, XML tags, and other tables to table cells. If you don't set a fixed row height, the height of a table row will grow to fit more lines of text after they have been added. It's not possible to add footnotes to tables.

These are the steps:

1. **Choose one of the following options while using the Type tool:**

   - After putting the entry point in a cell, the text should be typed in. Press either the Enter or Return key to start a new phrase in the same cell. You can move through the cells by pressing the Tab key. Pressing Tab in the last cell will start a new row. Click and hold on Shift and Tab to go back through the cells.

   - To paste the text, first copy it, then move the entry point to a cell and paste it. Then, go to Edit > Paste.

   - Choose File > Place, then double-click a text file. Then, put the entry point in the cell where you want to add text. This will let you add text right away.

Add graphics to a table

The steps are as follows:

1. You will need to place the entry point in the cell of the table where you want to add the image.

2. Choose one of the following options:

   - To choose one or more image files, from the menu, choose File > Place.

   - In the CC Libraries panel, pick out a few pictures from the pictures section. Then, drag and drop them where you want them to go. You can also look at the pictures on the placegun.

3. To put the picture or pictures you want to use, just click inside each table cell.
4. **Choose one of the following options:**

InDesign pieces that are in the Graphics section of the CC Libraries panel can't be moved around by dragging and dropping. If you add a picture that is bigger than the cell, the cell's height will grow to fit the picture. The cell's width will stay the same, though, and the image may go past the right edge of the cell. If the row where the graphic is placed is set to a specific height, the cell will be pushed out of line if the graphic is taller than the row height. This happens after the row height is set. If you move the picture outside of the table, change its size, and then copy and paste it into the cell that goes with the table, you can avoid having a cell that is overset. Using the following methods, you also have the option of adding pictures to table cells.

- You will be asked to set the settings after choosing **Object > Anchored Object > Insert**. After the fact, you can add a picture to the connected object.

- To paste a picture or frame, copy it first, then find where you want to put it, and finally choose **Edit > Paste** from the menu.

Add table headers and footers

If you make a long table, it can go past more than one column, frame, or even the whole page. By putting heads or footers in the right places, you can repeat the information at the top or bottom of each different part of the table.

The option to include rows for the header and footer is available when you build the table. You can also add rows for the header and footer and change how they are shown in the table in the Table Options dialog box. You can change the rows in the body to rows in the header or bottom.

Convert existing rows to header or footer rows

Here are the steps:

1. Pick the rows at the top of the table when you want to make header rows. The rows at the bottom of the table are where you can add footer rows.

2. From the drop-down menu, choose **Table > Convert Rows > To Header or Footer**.

Change header or footer row options

What to do:

1. Put the entry point inside the table and then choose **Table > Table Options > Headers and Footers** from the menu that comes up.

2. You should say how many rows are in the header or footer. You can add new rows to either the top or bottom of the table.

3. Say whether the information in the header or footer is shown in each text column (if the text frame has more than one), just once per frame, or only once per page.

4. Pick the right option if you don't want the header information to show up in the first row of the table. If you do not want the information about the footer to be shown in the very last row of the table, select the "**Skip Last**" option. When you want to show that the header or footer is longer, the **Skip First option** is very helpful because it lets you do that. Take the example of a table that goes across several pages. To make the opening text say "**Table 2 (Continued),**" select **Skip First** and then place Table 2 in the first row of the table. This is done so that the word "(Continued)" doesn't show up at the start of the table.

5. Click the "OK" button.

LONG DOCUMENT FEATURES

1. Open Adobe InDesign 2024 for the first time.

2. Access "**File**" > "**New**" > "**Book.**"

3. Click on the "**+**" sign in the Book panel.

4. Find the InDesign files that you want to use in your book and click on them.

5. Click "**Open**" to add them to the book.

6. The Book panel (Window > Book) shows all the files that are part of the book. You can move documents around the screen by dragging them to get the chapters or parts in the right order.

7. To make sure everything is the same, use master pages and modify styles in all of the book's papers. You can set up and change styles and master pages in a single document. To make these changes appear in all of your papers at the same time, right-click and select **"Sync All Documents."**

8. Use the **"Numbering & Section Options"** in the Pages panel to set up automatic page numbering. Put the **"Page Number"** marker on master pages to add page numbers.

9. To divide your book into parts, use the **"Start Section"** option in the Pages panel. For each part, you can add a different table of contents or use this to give each area a different numbering style.

10. A customizable TOC can be made with the **"Table of Contents"** feature. Based on the paragraph styles you choose; InDesign will update the TOC automatically when the content changes.

11. To make it easier to find your way around digital books and PDFs, add favorites. From the **"Hyperlinks"** panel, choose **"New Hyperlink Destination"** to make bookmarks.

12. To make changeable links, use cross-references in the text. If the page numbers change, InDesign will change any links to other parts or chapters immediately.

13. If your book needs an index entry, use the **"Index"** panel to make notes on index items. Pick the **"Generate Index"** option in the Index panel to make the index.

14. Use **"Package"** to get all of the related fonts and pictures in your paper into one zipped file. This is very important for printing or sharing, making sure that all the tools you need are available.

15. Use the right export options for each file (PDF, EPUB, etc.) to make sure the text is ideal for the result you want.

16. To keep track of all the different copies of your book, use dates or version numbers. Share individual files or the book file to work together.

17. Use the Preflight screen to look over the document for mistakes and missing information before you finish it. If you want to print your book, make sure your work meets the standards for print production by inspecting it before it leaves.

Managing lengthy documents with book features

1. **Create a Book File:**

   - Open Adobe InDesign and make a new book cover document.

   - Choose "File" > "New" > "Book..."

- Give the book file a name that makes sense.

2. **Add Documents to the Book:**

    - To add documents to the book, go to Window > Book and click on the "+" icon in the Book panel.

    - Pick out all the InDesign documents (chapters) you want to use and click "Open."

3. **Arrange Documents:** Drag the documents around in the Book panel to put them in the order you want.

4. **Page Numbering:** Make sure that the page numbers are the same in all of your papers. Pick "Numbering and Section Options" from the Book panel menu to set up how pages are numbered.

5. **Sync Styles and Swatches:** Make sure that all of your papers use the same paragraph styles, character styles, and swatches. To get styles and swatches to work together, use the "Sync" button in the Book panel.

6. **Master Pages:**

    - Use master pages to make sure that all of the book's headers, footers, and page sections look the same.

    - Change the master pages in one document, and then use "Sync" to make the changes appear in all of the books' documents.

7. **Table of Contents:** Use the Book panel to make a table of contents. It's time to add the TOC. To do this, go to "Layout" > "Table of Contents" and pick the book from the "Style" choice.

8. **Cross-References:** For changing links in a text, use cross-references. This is very helpful for citing tables, figures, or chapters.

9. **Footnotes and Endnotes:** Make sure that all of the footnotes and endnotes are managed the same way throughout the whole book. You can sync and change footnote and endnote settings in the Book panel.

10. **Indexing:** If your document needs an index, use the Book panel to make one and keep track of it. You can make an index that covers more than one document.

11. **Book Panel Options:** Look at the Book panel menu for more options. For example, "Export Book to PDF" lets you make a single PDF file from all the papers in the book.

12. **Preflight:** Use the Preflight screen often to look over your papers for mistakes or problems.

13. **Package for Printing or Distribution:** When you're ready to print or share the book, use the "File" > "Package" option to get all the linked files, fonts, and other things you need.

14. **Version Control:** Save different copies of your book file so you can keep track of changes and versions. To tell them apart, use version numbers or dates.

15. **Backup Regularly:** To avoid losing data, back up your book file and any other papers that are linked to it often.

CREATING AND UPDATING TABLES OF CONTENTS AND INDEXES

Create tables of contents in books

Before writing the table of contents for a book, make sure to do the following for the best results:

- Before you make a table of contents, make sure that the book list is complete, that all of the papers are mentioned in the right order, and that all of the headers have the correct paragraph styles.

- Make sure that all of the paragraphs in the book use the same style. Do not make papers with styles that have names that sound like they mean different things. If there is more than one style with the same name but different definitions, InDesign uses either the first instance of the style in the book or the style description found in the current document.

- If the necessary styles aren't available in the Table of Contents dialog box's pop-up options, you'll need to synchronize the book so that they are applied to the document that holds the table of contents.

- No chapter numbers should be used if you want number prefixes like 1-1, 1-3, and so on to show up in your table of contents. Instead, use section numbers. Part names can have a table of contents prefixes added to them.

CHAPTER 8: MANIPULATING IMAGES AND GRAPHICS

INSERT PICTURES AND IMAGES

Inserting Images Using the Place Command

The Place command is the main way that pictures are brought into InDesign. To use the **Place function to add a picture, do these things:**

1. Open your InDesign file and go to the page where you want to add the picture.

2. Click on "Place" in the "File" menu or press "Ctrl+D" (Windows) or "Cmd+D" (Mac) on your computer.

3. Find the place where you saved the picture file and click "Open."

4. The picture will now be in your cursor. You can click and drag to make a frame that fits the picture to the size you want.

WORKING WITH IMAGES IN INDESIGN

There are a number of tools and methods you can use to control and change your picture once it has been added to your document.

Resizing and Scaling Images

Follow these steps to change the size of a picture in InDesign:

- Use the "Selection Tool" (V) to choose the picture frame.

- To change the size of the frame, click and drag one of its handles. Hold down the "Shift" key while moving to keep the image's aspect ratio.

- In the "Control" or "Properties" panel, check the "Auto-Fit" box to make the picture fit the frame properly.

Adjusting Image Fitting Options

When it comes to putting pictures into their frames, InDesign gives you a number of options. To get to these options:

- Use the "Selection Tool" (V) to pick out the picture frame.

- To get to the fitting options, click the "Content Fitting" button in either the "Control" or "Properties" panel.

- Pick a fitting option from the drop-down menu, like "Center Content," "Fit Content Proportionally," or "Fill Frame Proportionally."

Formatting Image Frames

You can also change the look of picture frames by adding strokes, changing corner effects, and adding other visual effects:

- Use the "Selection Tool" (V) to pick out the picture frame.

- To change the stroke width, corner effects, and other formatting options, you can use the "Control" or "Properties" panel.

Managing Images in the Links Panel

InDesign's Links panel helps you keep track of all the pictures you've added to a project. To get to the Links panel, press "Window" and then "Links."

- You can update or relink pictures from this panel if their source files have changed.

- Look at things about the picture, like the file size, color mode, and resolution.

- Use the "Edit Original" function to open the picture in the program that made it so you can make more changes.

4 TIPS FOR WORKING WITH IMAGES IN INDESIGN

Tip 1: Use the Frame Fitting Options

When working with pictures in InDesign, it's important to make sure they fit right in their frames. Right-click on the picture frames and choose "Fitting" to get to the Frame Fitting Options. You can choose from different fitting options, like "Fit Content Proportionally," "Fill Frame Proportionally," or "Fit Content to Frame." This makes sure that your pictures keep their aspect ratio and don't look skewed or stretched.

Tip 2: Maintain Image Resolution

Maintaining the sharpness of your pictures is very important if you want to get good print results. The Links panel in InDesign tells you about the size of the pictures you've put, which helps you keep an eye on their quality. For print projects, you should aim for a resolution of at least 300 PPI. If you need to, you can use the "Relink" option in the Links panel to swap out low-resolution pictures for high-resolution ones.

Tip 3: Use Clipping Paths for Complex Image Shapes

Cut out the background of a picture with a complicated shape or place it where you want it. This will give your work a clean, professional look. You can use an image editor like Adobe Photoshop to make a clipping path, and then bring the picture into InDesign. Pick out the picture frame, click on the "Object" menu, pick "Clipping Path," and then pick the right path from the dropdown menu. This will make it easier for you to add the picture without any problems to your plan.

Tip 4: Use Libraries to Organize and Access Images

Using InDesign's Libraries tool, you can easily organize and get to your pictures. You can store and organize your pictures in libraries, which makes it easy to find them and use them in more than one document. You can make a new library by going to "File" and selecting "New > Library."

After that, you can drag and drop pictures from your computer or other InDesign files into the library to make it easy to find and use again. This makes your work easier and helps you stay consistent across all of your projects.

PLACING AND LINKING IMAGES FOR DYNAMIC UPDATES

You need to learn how to keep and update image links so that you can easily add graphics to your designs. When you add an image, a version of the file that fits the screen is shown in the plan. This lets you look at the picture and move it around in the plan. **There is a chance, though, that the real image file will be added or linked.**

- The artwork that is connected to the document is linked to it, but it still exists separately from the document. This makes the document smaller. Though transformation tools and effects can be used to make changes to linked artwork, it is not possible to pick out and change specific parts of the artwork. It is possible to use the linked picture in more than one way without making the page much bigger. One more thing that can be done is to change all the links at once. When you export or print, the original image is brought back to life. This means that the end output is made from the originals at their full quality.

- The artwork that is inserted is put into the page at its full size, which makes the paper bigger in the end. Your document is self-sufficient as long as the artwork is inserted; you can keep track of versions and make changes to the file whenever you want.

You can check the Links panel to see if the image is linked or embedded and to change its state from one to the other. Instead of the screen-quality version of a bitmap picture that you put into your layout that is 48K or less, InDesign will immediately use the full-resolution image. These pictures are shown in the Links panel by InDesign so that you can keep track of different versions and make changes to the file whenever you want. But you don't need the link for the best results. These pictures are shown in the Links panel by InDesign. Moving a document to a different folder or disk is important, like when you send it to a service provider. You must also move the picture files that go with the document. These files are not saved with the text. You can instantly copy all linked files when you use the Preflight and Package features.

Links panel overview

There is a list of all the files that have been added to a document in the Links panel. In this group are both files that are stored directly (on a disk) and assets that are managed on a computer. It is important to know that Internet Explorer does not show copied and pasted files from websites in this panel. The InCopy Links tab also shows items that are linked to each other. Find out about the number of notes, the controlled status, and the status of tracked changes in the Link Info area when you select a linked story in the Links panel. In this place, you can also see the status of tracked changes. If the same picture shows up more than once in the document, the links will be grouped together in the Links box and shown as a triangle with a disclosure triangle inside it. When an EPS or InDesign file that is linked has links, those links are also combined under a transparency triangle. This does happen in some situations. If the situation calls for it, the Links panel can show a related file in either of these ways:

Up to Date

When the file is up to date, the Status box is blank.

Modified

The version of the file in your document is older than the version that is saved on the disk if you see this indicator. For example, this signal will show up if you bring a picture you made in Photoshop into InDesign and then change it and save it in Photoshop. The people who do these things could be you or someone else. There is a slightly different form of the changed icon shown when an image is changed and some cases are updated but others are not. This happens when the image is edited.

Missing

Even though the picture might still be somewhere else, it is no longer at the site from which it was downloaded. Links can be lost if the source file is removed or if it is moved after being imported to a different computer or place. If the source file is not found, it is not possible to tell if a lost file is up to speed. If this icon is present, the file might not print or share at its full size if you try to do some of those things.

Embedded

While the contents of a linked file are being embedded, management steps for that connection are put on hold. There is an "edit in place" action happening on the given link right now that stops this option from being used. Management tasks will be able to be done on the link again after the file has been removed. If a linked object doesn't show up on a certain page of the document, the symbols PB (pasteboard), PP (parent page), OV (overset text), and HT (hidden text) will show you where the object is.

Use the Links Panel

- Choose **Window > Links** from the menu bar to open the Links panel. It is possible to tell them apart by the names of all the linked files and automatically inserted files.

- Right-click on a link in the Links panel and choose "Go to Link." This will take you to the linked image. You can click the link's page number in the Page column instead, or you can use the menu in the Links box to choose "Go to Link." The chosen picture takes up most of the space on the InDesign display. You have to show the layer (or condition, if the object is attached) before you can see a hidden object.

- Clicking the triangle icon to the left of the link will let you expand or break linked links. When the same graphic shows up more than once on a page or when the linked EPS graphic or InDesign file has links in it, nested links may appear in the document.

- To sort the links in the Links panel by category, click the category name at the top of the panel. This will arrange the panel's links in a certain order. If you click on the same group again, you can change the order. In this case, if you click on the Page group, the links will appear in the same order they were first shown, starting with the first page and ending with the last page. If you click Page again, the links will go from the most recent page to the most recent page. Panel Options can be used to make the Links panel have more grids.

WORK WITH THE LINKS PANEL COLUMNS

You can show more categories in the Links box if you want to tell people more about the images. Dimensions and Creation Date are two examples of these categories. You can pick whether the information is shown in the Links panel as a column or in the Link Info area at the bottom of the Links panel. **This is true for all of them.**

1. From the menu that shows up in the Links panel, choose **Panel Options**.

2. There are options under the Show Column heading that you can use to add columns to the Links panel. The linked file is in Folder 0, which is in turn contained within Folder 0. Folder 1 is also contained within Folder 0, and so on.

3. Pick out the boxes under the heading "Show in Link Info" to show the information in the "Link Info" part at the bottom of the panels for links.

4. Press the OK button.

You will be able to change the order of the columns if you pick a column and then drag it to a new spot. You can change the width of the column by moving the column edges. Click on the name of the group you want to sort the links by to see them in ascending order. Click again to put the things in decreasing order.

Change the Links panel rows and thumbnails

What to do:

1. From the menu that shows up in the Links panel, choose **Panel Options**.

2. There are three Row Size options: Small Rows, Regular Rows, and Large Rows.

3. In the Name column and the Link Info area at the bottom of the Links panel, you can choose whether thumbnails of the images are shown. You can use this option for the Thumbnails tool.

4. Press the OK button.

WORKING WITH VECTOR GRAPHICS

Placing Vector Graphics:

1. **Launch InDesign:** Open or make a new document in Adobe InDesign to start working with vector graphics.

2. **Importing Vector Files:**

- To place something, go to the File menu and select "Place," or press Ctrl + D on a Windows computer or Cmd + D on a Mac computer.

- Pick out the vector file you want to use and click "Open."

Scaling and Transforming:

3. **Scaling Vector Graphics:** To change the size of vector images, use the Selection Tool (V). Hold down the Shift key and drag the corner handles to keep the scale proportional.

4. **Rotating or Skewing:** Hover over a corner with the Selection Tool until the rotation icon shows up. You can now rotate or skew the vector image.

Making Changes to Vector Graphics:

5. **Entering Isolation Mode:** Use the Selection Tool to double-click on the added vector image to go into an isolated mode where you can make changes.

6. **Editing Anchor Points:** To select particular anchor points, use the Direct Selection Tool (A). When you're in isolation mode, use the Pen Tool (P) to add, remove, or change lines.

Working with Layers:

7. **Layers Panel:**

   - The Layers Panel (Window > Layers) lets you change how your document is organized.

   - Change how vector drawings are shown and stacked since they are on different layers.

Using Color and Stroke:

8. **Color Adjustment:** To change the colors of vector drawings, go to Window > Color > Swatches or Window > Color > Color.

9. **Stroke Characteristics:** Use the Stroke Panel (Window > Stroke) to make any changes you need to the stroke properties.

10. **Embedding and Linking:** While working with InDesign, you have the option to embed or connect vector images. Embedding makes the file bigger, but it will still be movable. Linking, on the other hand, keeps a link to the original file.

Exporting with Vector Graphics:

11. **Exporting:**

   - When you want to export your InDesign project, make sure you pick a file that works with vectors, like PDF.

   - You should also make sure that the "Preserve Illustrator Editing Capabilities" option is set if you need to make more changes in Illustrator.

If you follow these steps, you'll be able to work quickly with vector drawings in Adobe InDesign. You can import and transform them, make fine changes, and organize their levels.

Editing vector graphics within InDesign

Like Adobe Illustrator, InDesign is not a full-fledged vector graphics editor, but it does let you do some things that you need to do for vector editing.

1. After starting Adobe InDesign, you can make a new project or open an old one.

2. Go to **File** > **Place** in the "Place" menu to choose your vector image file, such as an AI, EPS, or PDF file.

3. You have to click on the page first to move the picture. Use the Selection Tool (V) to move and change its size.

Basic Editing of Vector Files

1. You should use the Direct Selection Tool (A) to pick out specific anchor points or lines in the vector graphic.

2. You can change the size and rotation of the whole visual document with the Selection Tool. Holding down the Shift key will keep the proportions the same while you scale.

3. You can group multiple objects that you have chosen by using the **Object** > **Group** menu option. To separate, go to **Object** > **Ungroup**.

4. If you go to **Window > Object & Layout > Pathfinder**, you can see the Pathfinder screen. This panel lets you do basic things like adding, removing, combining shapes, and more.

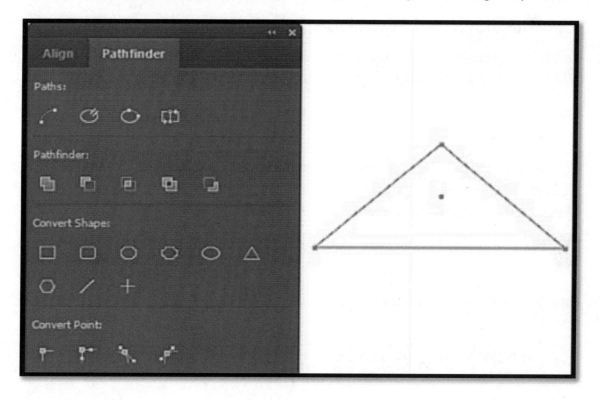

Stroke and Fill

1. Stroke and Fill options can be found in either the Control panel or the Swatches panel. They can be used to change how the vector image looks.

2. To add stripes and change the clarity, use the Gradient panel and the Effects panel.

Text and Vector Integration

1. The Type Tool (T) is what you should use to add text to your work. No problems can come up when text and vector images are put together.

2. It's possible to write in creative ways with the Type on a Path Tool because it lets you put text along a vector path.

Exporting

Go to the **File** menu and select **Export** to save or send your changes to a PDF, EPS, or any other file type that is easy to access.

Limitations

- When you compare InDesign's vector work to professional vector tools like Adobe Illustrator, it doesn't have as many features. If you want to make complicated graphic art, you should use Illustrator first and then load the idea into InDesign.

- You can use some live effects in InDesign, but to make more complex effects and filters, you should use Illustrator or Photoshop first and then bring the final design into InDesign.

IMAGE MANIPULATION TECHNIQUES

1. To choose your picture, go to **File** > **Place** and click on it. That's not all—you can easily add the picture to your InDesign page by dragging and dropping it.

2. Before moving on, the Place dialog box lets you pick the right options, such as cropping and fitting.

3. To make the picture you choose, click on it. Basic changing options like Cropping, Rotating, and Flipping Horizontally or vertically can only be accessed by going to the **Object** menu and selecting **Image**.

4. Through the **Effects** panel, you can change things like brightness, contrast, color, and more.

5. Pick out the picture from the **Window** menu, and then pick out **Effects** to get to the Effects panel.

6. Find the **Adjustments** drop-down menu below the "fx" sign at the bottom of the screen. This will let you change the image's color and tone.

7. You can make different visual effects by changing a picture's clarity or by using different blending modes.

8. To set blending modes or transparency, open the **Effects** panel, click on the "fx" button, and pick **Transparency** from where the choices appear.

9. You can use either the Pen tool or the shape tools to make a shape over the picture. Make sure both the picture and the form are chosen, then right-click on the picture and pick "Make Clipping Mask."

10. You should make picture frames and then move them around if you want to have more control over where photos are placed.

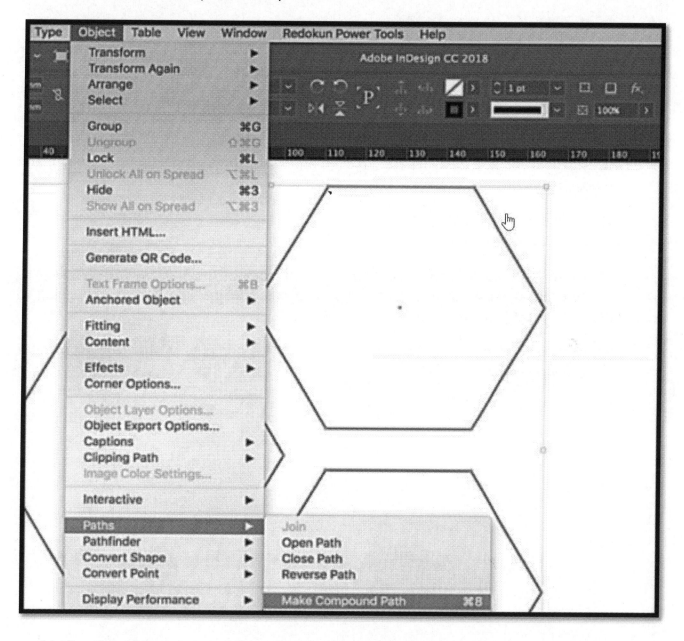

11. You should first make a frame with the "Rectangle" or "Ellipse" tool and then put a picture inside it.

12. InDesign lets you connect to picture files stored outside of InDesign. If the picture that is

linked to is modified, InDesign will add the new version right away.

13. Press "File" and then "Place" to pick out the picture. Make sure the "Link" option is chosen in the Place dialog box.

14. InDesign lets you add many different picture effects, such as drop shadow, highlight and emboss and more.

15. Pick out the picture you want to change, then go to "Window" > "Effects" and pick the "fx" icon from the list that comes up.

16. Make sure that the resolution of your photos is high enough that the quality of the pictures will stay the same when you print them. You can see the image's size by going to "Window" > "Info" in the menu bar.

17. You have the option to export pictures in a specific file and quality when you export your InDesign document.

CHAPTER 9: MASTERING COLOR IN YOUR DESIGNS

APPLYING COLOR TO TEXT AND OBJECTS

Color is an important tool for designers, but it can be hard for new users to figure out how to use it in InDesign. InDesign's color options can act erratically at first while you're still getting used to how everything works. This is very annoying and stops you from getting work done. When you're not used to the program, one of the most annoying things can be changing the color of the font. No matter how crazy InDesign seems, there is a method to its madness. Knowing how text color works in InDesign will help you understand and work better with text in InDesign.

Text Contents vs. Text Frame

It is important to know that InDesign sees the text frame and the text inside the frame as two separate objects when you change the color of the text in it. You can change the background color of both the text frame and the text itself to a different color. This is where most people get lost because if you choose a color for the text frame, it will instead be added to the text itself.

There will always be two options when applying color to a text frame in InDesign: formatting affects the container (shown by the left arrow above), and formatting affects the text (shown by the right arrow above). To change the color of text in InDesign, you need to know the difference between those two things. But there's still one more thing that makes it hard to use. You will have to use the Type tool to pick the text inside the container if your text frame is tied to another text frame. The Formatting affects text option will not work if you choose the frame. You can pick a lot of text from several linked text boxes by placing the text cursor inside the text frame and pressing Command + A (or Ctrl + A on a PC).

Changing Color Using the Tools Panel

There are color swatches at the bottom of the Tools panel that make it easy to change the color of text in InDesign. To begin, choose the text or text frame that you want to colorize. Keep in mind that if your text frame is linked, you'll need to use the Type tool to pick the text itself instead of just the text frame.

Click the small capital letter T button below the color choices while a text frame is chosen to go to the Formatting affects text mode. If you pick text directly, the Tools box should change to Formatting affects text mode immediately. The color bars will also have a capital T in the middle, as shown below.

If you double-click on the Fill swatch (shown above), the Color Picker dialog box will appear. Click OK after picking the color you want to use. The color of the text you chose will change to match the new one.

Changing Text Color Using the Color Panel

You can also use the Color panel in InDesign to change the color of text, though you might need to set it up first based on how your workspace is set up. You can show the Color panel if you open the Window menu and choose Color on the list of options. With the Type tool, choose the text you want to colorize. Then, open the Color panel.

Click the panel menu button (shown above) to open the Color panel menu. Then, choose the color space that works best for your project. Print projects usually use the CMYK colorspace, while screen-based projects use the RGB colorspace. However, you can mix colors in any way you want, since they will all be changed to the correct color space before being exported.

If it applies, make sure that the Color panel is set to Formatting affects text. Then, move each slider until you get the color you want. Instead of starting the Color Picker for every small change, this can be a much easier way to make color changes in your plan.

Using Swatches for Consistent Text Color

If you need to change the color of text across a long document or just want to make sure that all of your text colors are the same, you should become familiar with the Swatches panel. With swatches, you can save colors you use often in a document so you don't have to type them in again every time. This can save you a lot of time.

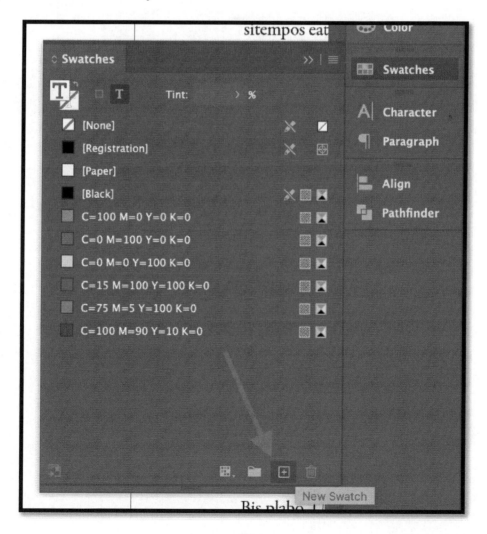

Creating new swatches can be done in a few different ways. You can open the Swatches panel, click the "New Swatch" button at the bottom of the panel, and then double-click your new swatch to make changes to it. Alternatively, you can open the Color Picker dialog window and click the "Add CMYK Swatch" button. Choose the text or text frame you want to use the swatch on, make sure the Swatches panel is set to Formatting affects text mode, and then click on the swatch you want to use. The new color will be used in your text.

Change the Color of Multiple Text Boxes

Using paragraph styles and color swatches is the only way to change the color of text in several text boxes that are not linked to each other. Once you've assigned a style to each paragraph, you can change the style in one place, and all the paragraphs that use that style will update to match. Paragraph styles are similar to style templates for text. Basic Paragraph is the name of the basic paragraph style that will be used in all of the text frames you make in InDesign.

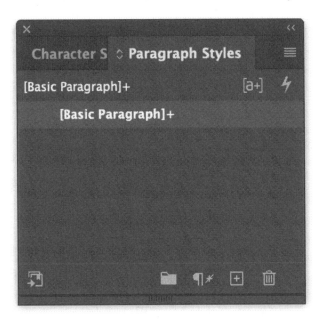

To begin, make a swatch for the color you want to use by following the steps we talked about earlier. Next, open the Paragraph Styles panel. To see the style options, double-click the item that says "Basic Paragraph."

Choose Character Color from the list on the left side of the Paragraph Style Options box. From the list, choose the swatch you made earlier.

WHY IS MY INDESIGN TEXT HIGHLIGHTED IN BLUE?

If your InDesign text is being highlighted in light blue by accident, you won't be able to change it with the color settings in this post because the text isn't colored. When you see light blue text, that's just InDesign telling you that local formatting has been used to override a paragraph style.

You can turn this off in the Paragraph Styles panel, but it helps to find local formatting in long documents. Toggle Style Override Highlighter is the first item on the menu in the Paragraph Styles box.

SPOT COLORS AND COLOR LIBRARIES

- A color-matching method, like the Pantone Matching method (PMS), is often used to choose spot colors.

- A different recipe is used to make each spot color, which makes sure that the colors are the same in all printing methods.

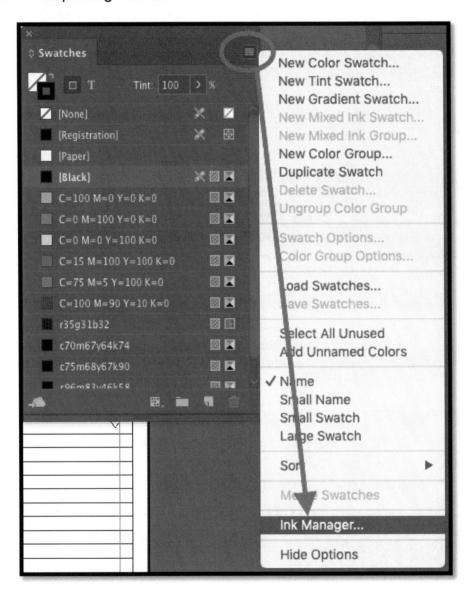

Creating Your Document

- Open Adobe InDesign 2024 and either make a new document or open an old one.

- Go to *File -> Document Setup* to check and change your document's color mode. *Spot Color* is great for spot colors.

Using the Swatches Panel

If you want to see the Swatches panel, go to *Window -> Color -> Swatches*.

Adding Spot Colors

To add spot colors, click the *New Swatch* button at the bottom of the Swatches screen.

- Choose *Spot* as the color type and a selection of spot color libraries, like Pantone.

- Click *Add* or *OK* to add the spot color you chose to your samples.

Using Spot Colors on Objects

- Pick out an object or piece of text that you want to apply a spot color.

- Pick out the spot color swatch you need in the Swatches box.

Checking for Separations

- To make sure your spot colors are applied correctly, go to *View* and then *Overprint Preview*.

- You can see the separations by going to *Window -> Output -> Separations Preview*.

Adding Special Effects

- Give the objects with spot colors extra effects like gradients, transparency, or effects.

- Use the *Effects* tab to give the picture glows, drop shadows, and other effects.

Exporting for Print

- If you want to export your work, go to *File -> Export*.

- Check that the file is in a format that can be printed, like PDF, and make sure that *Include Spot Colors* is checked in the export options if it's there.

Using Printers to Communicate

- Make sure your printer can handle spot colors by checking with them.

- Give them a colorproof or swatch book to help them match the colors you want properly.

- Check a copy after printing to make sure the spot colors and special effects are printed the way you want them to be.

CHAPTER 10: CREATING INTERACTIVE DOCUMENTS

CREATING HYPERLINKS AND CROSS-REFERENCES

Setting up Text Anchors in your InDesign project and then making a cross-reference to the anchor is a simple process that lets you make documents with a strong and clear related structure. **The process of making a cross-reference to where a text link is located is split into two steps:**

- Make sure the text link is placed where the goal text should be.

- Place the cross-reference at the start of the source text.

To create the text anchor:

1. Go to the part of the page that the cross-reference text is pointing to.

2. You can either click to place the text entry point or drag over some text to make it stand out.

3. The Cross-Reference box can be seen from the menu bar by going to **Window -> Type and Tables -> Cross-References**.

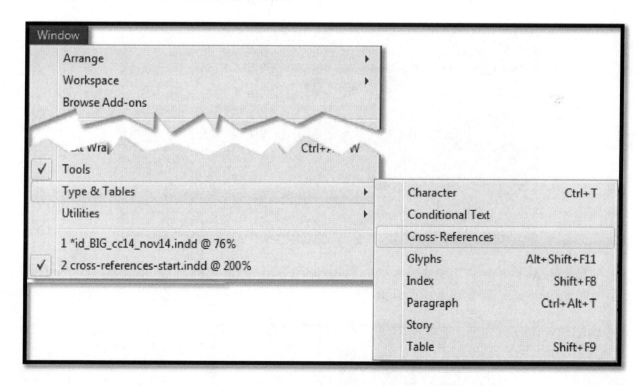

4. In the Cross-References box, choose **New Hyperlink Destination** from the list of options that come up.

5. A dialogue box for the New Hyperlink Destination appears. For some reason, the Type pop-up option is always set to Text Anchor. If you select some text and then click on the **New Hyperlink Destination** command, that text will stay in the Name field during the whole process. In the Name box, you have the option of giving the text anchor a name. This will make it easy to find if you didn't highlight the text.

6. If the Show Hidden Characters switch is on, a text anchor sign will appear in front of the text you chose. To move on, click OK.

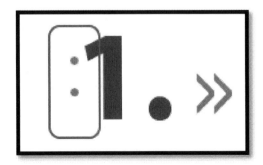

Follow these steps to make a cross-reference to a text anchor:

1. Go to the place in the document where you want to add the cross-reference. Next, go to the starting point. An example of the first text that should be used for the cross-reference is "(see)"

2. Second, you need to make sure that the text entry point is exactly where you want the cross-reference text that was made instantly to show up.

3. Find the Cross-Reference panel's menu. Turn on the option to Insert Cross-Reference.

4. In the New Cross-Reference dialog box, choose *Text Anchor* from the list of options that come up for Link To.

5. If the target for the cross-reference is not in the currently open document, use the Document pop-up menu to choose the right one.

6. Take a text anchor that you've already made and choose it from the Text Anchor pop-up menu.

7. Choose the words that will be in the cross-reference by clicking on one of the options in the window that pops up after you click on Format.

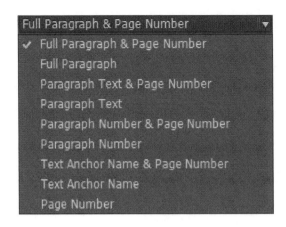

8. When you click the OK button, the cross-reference text and the "page #" markings show up at the Text insertion location. If the "Show Hidden Characters" option is chosen, a cross-reference box will appear around the page number. Also, if the text in your document moves around, the cross-reference page number that is made automatically will be changed to represent the new location of the content that is being cross-referenced.

Creating Cross-References

1. Make sure you know how the cross-reference text should be formatted before you start making them. Go to **Type > Cross-References** to make new formats for pages, parts, or figures.

2. To enter the cross-reference, move the mouse to the desired spot, then go to **Type > Cross-References**, select the appropriate table style, and then click **"Insert."**

3. To make connections, follow the steps we talked about before, but this time use the cross-reference marking as the location.

4. You can update cross-references if you make changes to your text by going to **Type > Update Cross-References.** This makes sure that cross-references are correct and show the most up-to-date information.

5. Save your work as a PDF file, and then check the cross-references to make sure they go to the right places.

Linking content for seamless navigation

1. Click **"Window" > "Interactive" > "Hyperlinks"** to open the Hyperlinks panel.

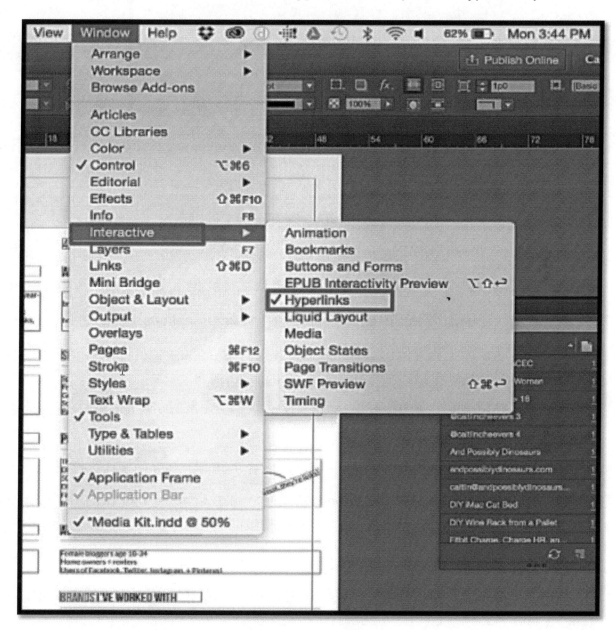

2. Pick out the text or object you want to turn into a hyperlink.

3. In the Hyperlinks panel (the chain icon is at the bottom of the panel), click the **"New Hyperlink"** button. Another option is to right-click on the text or object you want to link to and choose **"New Hyperlink."**

4. You can connect to a number of places from the Hyperlink Destination text box, such as:

- Use the **"Page"** option to link to a specific page in your text.

- **URL:** A URL is a web address that leads to a website.

- Use the **"File"** option to link to another file or document.

- **Text Anchor:** This function lets you link to a specific anchor point on the page.

5. Once you've chosen the location, you can pick from other options, such as:

- **Appearance:** Here you can choose how the hyperlink will look, like making it stand out by underlining it or changing its color.

- **Highlight:** Use the **"Highlight"** function to choose how the link will look when the mouse is moved over it.

6. You have to go through the steps again if you want to make more hyperlinks.

7. If you want your control buttons to be clickable, make shapes and then turn them into buttons. Simply select the shape, then select **"Window" > "Interactive" > "Buttons"** as the menu option to access the Buttons and Forms panel. Alter the shape so that it looks like a button and set its actions, like "Go to Page."

8. Export your file as a dynamic PDF so you can check the links. Go to **"File" > "Export"** and select Adobe PDF (Interactive) to customize the options. After that, save the changes.

9. The PDF that was made should be opened, and the hyperlinks should be checked by clicking on the text or objects that are linked.

10. The Table of Contents function in InDesign is something you might want to use if your document is broken up into several parts. Since this is the case, you can automatically make links to different parts of your text.

CROSS-REFERENCING WITHIN AND ACROSS DOCUMENTS

Cross-References within a Document

1. First, load your InDesign file to get into it. Figure out which parts of the information you want to cross-reference, such as the headers, figures, or tables.

2. Moving the mouse to where you want the cross-reference to show up is step two. When you go to Type, a choice will show up. Choose **Cross-References** from that list. You can choose what kind of reference you want to use in the Cross-References panel. For example, you can choose to use a paragraph, page number, or picture.

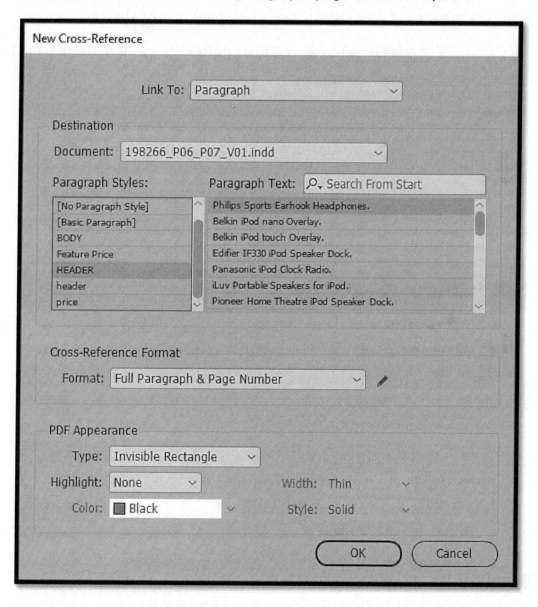

3. Pick out the thing from the list that will be the source, and then click **"Insert."**

4. You can change the way cross-references look by changing the character style that is related to them. Click on **"Character Style"** in the Cross-References window to write your character.

5. If the content changes, you can update the cross-references by selecting them and then clicking the **"Update"** button in the Cross-References box.

Cross-References across Documents

- Go to **File > New > Book** to make a book file for projects that have a lot of InDesign files.

- By clicking the **"Add Document"** button in the Book panel, you can add your files to the book file.

- To start, go to **Window > Book** and open the Book tab. Double-check that the papers are written in the right way. To make cross-references, paragraph styles, and character styles the same in all of your papers, use the **"Synchronize Options"** option.

- In the Cross-References box, use the **"Book"** dropdown menu to choose the document you want to use as a reference. This is the same process you would use inside a document. To use the paper, you will need to do this.

- To change cross-references between all the files in a book, go to the book panel's options menu and choose **"Update References."**

ADDING BUTTONS AND FORMS

Creating Buttons

1. Enter Adobe InDesign and either make a new project or enter an old one.

2. Lay out your paper and style it the way you usually would. Make sure you leave room for things that can be engaged with.

3. To open the Buttons and Forms panel, go to the **"Window"** menu and choose **"Interactive > Buttons and Forms"** from the list. Click on the **"Button"** tool in the panel

to choose it.

4. Just click and drag to add a button anywhere on your page. In the Buttons and Forms panel, you can give the button a name, change how it looks, and change how it is laid out.

5. There are three different states that buttons can be in: normal, rollover, and click. The **"States"** panel is where you can change how each state looks. Adding effects like changing the color or the transparency is a good way to make the mood engaging and changing.

6. Go to the Buttons and Forms panel and click on it to get to the **"Actions"** tab. Choose the time the action should happen from the **"Event"** dropdown menu. For example, "On Click." Choose the action you want to take from the **"Action"** dropdown menu. For example, **"Go to Next Page"** or **"Show/Hide Buttons."**

Creating Forms

- When you're making forms, use the **"Text Field"** tool to make a text field where people can enter text.

- To change how the Buttons and Forms panel looks, you can set a default number and change how the panel looks overall.

- The **"Checkbox"** or **"Radio Button"** tool for drawing should be used to make checks or radio buttons.

- You need to give each checkbox and radio button a name in the Buttons and Forms panel to show how they work.

- **"Dropdown"** is the tool you should use to make a dropdown list. You can add things to the list that is shown on the screen in the Buttons and Forms panel.

- Put a button on the page and set its action to **"Submit Form"** to make a button that can be used to send that form. The function of a button that clears the form should be set to **"Reset Form."**

- When you use the **"Text"** tool and place the text close to the interactive elements, you can add instructions or tooltips to help users find their way.

Exploring form field options and functionalities

1. Open Adobe InDesign and make a new project or use one that you already have.

2. To get to the "Interactive" panel, open the "Window" menu and choose the "Interactive" option. In the "Interactive" panel, click on "Forms" to see the form's choices.

3. Open your file and choose the "Type Tool" from the toolbar. Simply click and drag the text frame to place it where you want the form space to show up. When you're done choosing

the text frame, go to the "Interactive" panel and find the "Buttons and Forms" choice.

4. Decide what kind of form field you want to make. It could be a Text Field, Checkbox, Radio Button, Dropdown List, or Text Field.

5. You can change the features of a text field that you have chosen in the "Text Field Properties" window. There are two ways to get to the properties: right-click or double-click on the text field and choose "Text Field Options." You can change things like the maximum length of the text, how it looks, and how it is formatted.

6. Set specific settings for radio buttons and checkboxes, such as the export value, the default state, and how they appear. You should double-click on the selection or radio button to get to its settings.

7. You can make a dropdown list by selecting "Dropdown" from the "Buttons and Forms" menu. You can change the list's features, like the font and appearance, as well as the things that are in it.

8. You can also add activities to form areas to make them more dynamic. Once you've chosen the form field in the "Buttons and Forms" panel, click the "Add New Action" button during the process. Choose the action that will be taken (like "Go to Next Page" or "Show/Hide Button") and the event that will set it off (like "On Focus," "On Blur," or "On Mouse Up").

9. To test the form fields, go to "File" > "Export" and choose "Adobe PDF (Interactive)." You should open the exported PDF in a PDF reader that can handle interactive features in order to test your form fields.

10. Don't forget to use the "Preview" panel to see how your interactive features work. The "Articles" panel and grouping form areas that are linked to each other can be used to change the order of the interactive elements.

11. Make sure your forms are easy to find by giving the spaces on them the right names or labels. You can change things about form fields, like the alternate text, in the "Accessibility" panel.

12. You have to save your InDesign project often to keep the dynamic parts up to date. The live PDFs should be shared with other people so that they can fill them out online.

CONFIGURING SETTINGS FOR INTERACTIVE EXPORTS

Method 1: Prepare your Document

- Make sure that the layout of your paper is set up so that it can be interactive. You can add any other interactive elements you want, like buttons, hyperlinks, and video elements that let users interact with the content itself.

- You should use hyperlinks in your text whenever they are needed. They can lead to other pages in the same document, websites that are not in the same document, or email addresses.

- Create interactive buttons in the "Buttons and Forms" panel and give them functions like "Go to Page" or "Open URL." This screen has a button that you can click on to do something.

- Additionally, if your paper has multimedia elements like pictures or music, you need to make sure that they are properly attached or linked.

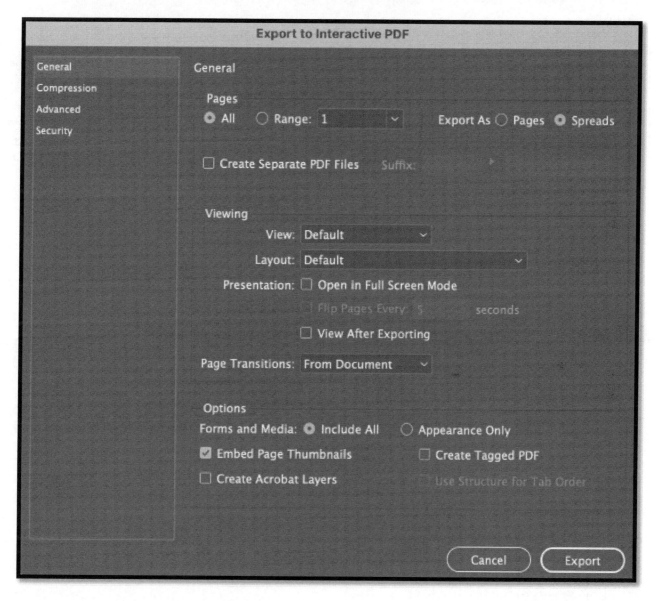

Method 2: Access the Export Options

- To save the file in a different format, go to "File" > "Export" or press Cmd + E (Mac) or Ctrl + E (Windows).

- During the download process, you will need to pick the file you want to use. If you want your document to have both print and interactive parts, choose "Adobe PDF (Interactive)" or "Adobe PDF (Print)" for interactive documents.

Method 3: Configuring the Interactive Export Settings

- Make sure the "Adobe PDF Preset" is set to "High-Quality Print" or pick a different preset that works for you.

- If you need to, pick the right page range.

- You can change the picture compression settings to fit the needs of your paper.

- Setting the crop marks, bleed, and any other print-related choices should be done whenever it's needed.

- Make sure that the "Include Hyperlinks" choice is selected to make sure that the hyperlinks are kept in the saved PDF. Use the "Include" menu to choose the right choices for buttons and forms if you have them.

- Customizing any extra advanced choices will help you make them fit your needs.

Method 4: Export the Document

- Pick a name and a place for the file to be exported.

- If you want to make the interactive PDF, click the "Export" button.

Method 5: Test the Interactive Elements

- Open the produced PDF file in Adobe Acrobat or any other PDF reader that can show interactive elements.

- Please make sure that the hyperlinks work the way they should. Make sure that when you click on the buttons, they do what you want them to do.

- If your project has multimedia parts, you should check that the movies and music work the way you want them to.

Consider the following further suggestions:

- If you want to include navigational bookmarks, set them up in your InDesign document before you export it.

- Think about accessibility by adding alternate text to pictures and making sure that people who can help can access the engaging parts.

CHAPTER 11: COLLABORATING WITH ADOBE INCOPY

INCOPY INTEGRATION

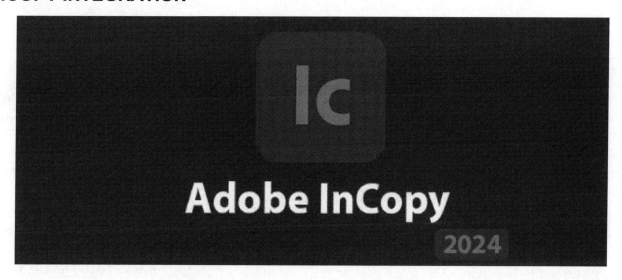

The word processor InCopy is great, and the fact that it works with InDesign makes working together easier. Adobe InCopy lets you change text without changing the way the publication is laid out. This gives the author, editor, or reviewer control over the text and it gives the artist control over how the page looks. Also, they can work on the same document at the same time, like when they're on the same local network. So, whether you are working alone or with a group on an InDesign job, InCopy is a great tool that you should check out.

Install and set up InCopy

Are you excited to use Adobe InCopy for the first time? Here are the steps you need to take to get it going on your computer:

1. Install Adobe Creative Cloud first. You will need to use Adobe Creative Cloud first because Adobe InCopy is part of that suite. For those who don't already have it, you can download it from Adobe's website.

2. Once Adobe Creative Cloud is loaded on your computer, you'll be able to find InCopy in the list of programs you can use. As soon as you click the "Install" button next to InCopy, the Creative Cloud app will handle the rest. It might take a few minutes to finish the installation process.

3. Get your work area ready. As soon as you have loaded InCopy, you can change your workspace to fit your needs. Open the "Window" tab and pick "Workspace." You can choose a current workspace or make your own from this page.

4. You'll need to link InCopy to InDesign if you work with people who use InDesign. From the "File" menu, choose "New." Then, choose "Document from InDesign template." Finally, find the InDesign file you want to work with. You will be able to do the job.

Collaborative editing with InCopy

1. Share your InDesign file with your team. This is the first thing you need to do to work together. This has to be done to make working together easier. You can do this by putting it as a task in a place that everyone on your team can see.

2. Open the file in InCopy. After that, everyone on the team will be able to open the file. They can choose to open the whole task or just certain parts of it.

3. Once you've opened the file, you can make any changes you want and then save them. It's built into InCopy to remember to save any changes you make to the shared spot while you work. Because of this, the people on your team will be able to see your changes right away.

4. Check out and check in. There is a check-in/check-out feature in InCopy that keeps files from being changed. If you choose to check out an item, no one else can read it until you choose to check it back in. This way, everyone can work on the paper at the same time without getting in the way of each other.

MANAGING INCOPY ASSIGNMENTS AND WORKFLOWS

InDesign is the "master" that controls the whole process for both InDesign and InCopy. InDesign is used to make the layout, and it also uses InCopy content to it, then InCopy would only be a text editor and not be able to make page layouts.

Here are some of the most important things that InDesign does during the process:

- Users of InDesign are responsible for using InCopy to add content to a layout.

- People who use InDesign have to put text and picture frames inside a page layout so that people who use InCopy can work without being stopped.

- After the layout is made, the text and picture frames are assigned to it so that InCopy can access its information.

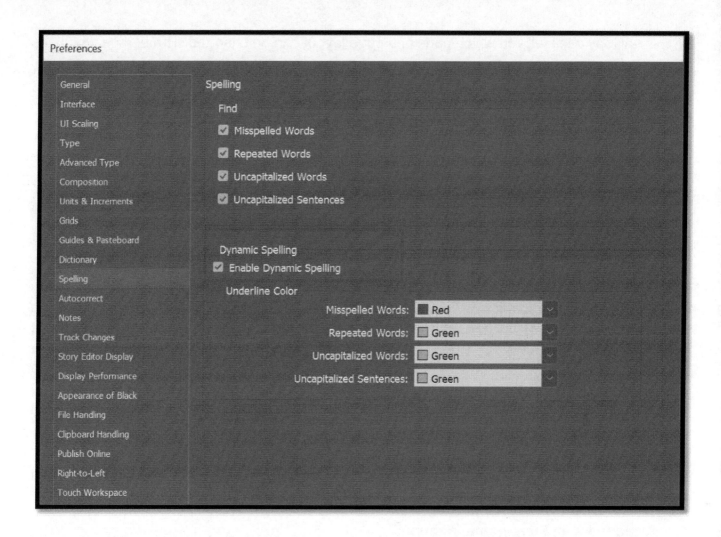

InCopy's Role in the Workflow

InCopy is a text editor that lets you import and place pictures. It is the part of the process that is in charge of editing. InCopy can use layouts that have already been made, but it can't make layouts itself. It can work with material in layouts, on the other hand. You can also use it to write text (called a "manuscript") that you can then load into InDesign. One of the benefits of writing the text in InCopy instead of Microsoft Word is that nothing is lost when it is sent from InCopy to InDesign. As the editor or author works in InCopy, they can see how the file will be imported into InDesign. In the early stages of the process, you can switch styles to make the copy fit better.

Here's a rundown of some of the most useful features of InCopy:

- Text, tables, and other features can be worked with in the same way that InDesign can be used. It is possible to use styles to make the switch from InCopy to InDesign go more smoothly than the usual way, which is to go from Microsoft Word to InDesign.

- InCopy can be used to make new text files. This helps when it comes to putting together the words. InDesign users, on the other hand, are free to add that text to a layout however they want.

- Please note that InCopy can only change text and images that are part of an InDesign layout if the user has directly chosen to do so.

- InCopy can't tell you which parts of a page layout can be changed. The person who uses InDesign makes the choice.

- When you use InCopy on a layout that was made just for it, the software can change the text. You can copy other people's work, but you can't change it.

- It's not possible for InCopy to make a text/picture frame for newly made files. The only things that InDesign can handle are things that are already in frames that it made.

- InCopy can add pictures to picture frames that are already there if an InDesign user has given it permission to do so.

Versioning and Collaboration Best Practices

Versioning and collaboration are important parts of using Adobe InDesign, especially when working on design projects with other people and adding to a single document. **Here are a lot of the best ways to work together and keep track of versions in Adobe InDesign:**

1. **File Organization:**

    - Make sure your InDesign project's folders are clear and well-organized. Put source files, pictures, and other items in their own folders.

    - Make sure that the names of your files and folders are uniform and detailed so that they are easy to find.

2. **Save As an Incremental Naming:**

- Use "Save As" often to make copies of your InDesign file that are bigger than the last one. This lets you keep track of changes and quickly go back to an earlier version if you need to.

- Put a version number or date in the title so that you can quickly see what state the document is in.

3. **Master Pages for Consistency:** Use master pages to make sure that your whole work is consistent. This makes sure that changes made to a master page are made to the whole text, so there are fewer chances of mistakes.

4. **Collaborative Workflows:**

    - When working on a project with other people, make sure everyone knows their clear jobs and duties. Make it clear who is in charge of which parts or pieces of the design.

    - You might want to use Adobe's InCopy for collaborative text editing, which lets artists and copywriters work on the same page at the same time.

5. **Linked Assets:** Instead of adding pictures and graphics, link them to other files. This keeps the size of the InDesign file doable and lets team members change images that

are tied to the main page without changing it.

6. **Package and Share:**

   - Use InDesign's "Package" tool on a regular basis to put all of your linked files, fonts, and the InDesign document itself in one place. This makes it easy to share with clients or coworkers.

   - Use a version-controlled tool to share the packed folder so that everyone is working with the same files.

7. **Version Control Systems:** If you work with a lot of people, you should use version control systems like Git or SVN as part of your process. This lets you keep track of changes, handle issues, and go back to earlier versions if you need to.

8. **Communication Channels:**

   - Make sure your team has clear ways to talk to each other. Keep each other up to date on progress, changes, and problems on a regular basis to keep the process running smoothly.

   - To keep conversations and file sharing in one place, use project management tools or contact platforms.

9. **Make regular backups:** Set up a strong backup plan. Back up your InDesign project often so that you don't lose any data if something goes wrong or the system crashes.

10. **Documentation:** Keep detailed records of the project's structure, design choices, and any special directions for team members. This helps new people on the team understand the job right away.

CHAPTER 12: PREPARING DOCUMENTS FOR PRINTING

PREFLIGHTING AND DOCUMENT VERIFICATION

A big part of the InDesign editing process is preflight, which is used to fix technical problems like lost pictures or fonts or text that is too close to the edge of the page. There is an open InDesign file here.

At first glance, everything seems to be fine. In the bottom left area of the screen, though, there is a small red circle next to some writing that says "3 errors." There are problems with the paper that need to be fixed before you send it to print if there is a red circle here.

If you double-click on the red circle, you can get to the Preflight panel. You can also get to the Preflight panel from the main menu by going to **Window > Output > Preflight**. First, there is a check box in the upper left corner of the screen that lets you turn Preflight On or off. Pre flight should always be on, just in case. This means that as you work, InDesign will actively point out technical mistakes and change them to "No errors" as you fix them.

In the middle of the screen is the Error window. This page is where Preflight shows and sorts the mistakes it has found. There is a missing link, as shown in the error message that grows when you click the gray line to the left of the text. If you click the gray line again, you'll see the name of the missing link. It will take you right to the link in your project if you double-click on its name.

Click to choose the link's name in the Preflight panel. Then, click to open the Info window at the bottom of the panel. InDesign is trying to help you by telling you exactly what's wrong and how to fix it. To find the lost file, go to the Links panel and click the "Relink" button. The Relink button, which looks like a chain link, is at the bottom of the top part of the Links panel. If the link is missing, it will be marked with a red question mark.

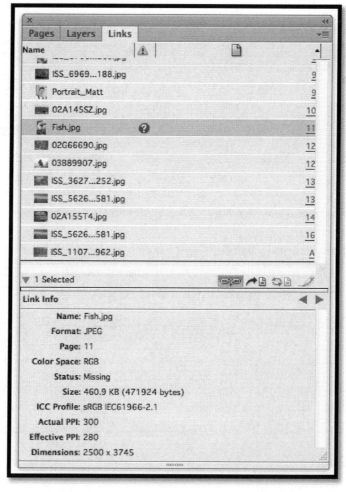

This is where you can find the broken link and click Open to fix it. Now the missing link is fixed, and you can see in the Preflight panel that the error message is gone. I only have two more problems to solve.

The last few mistakes have to do with text. To find out more about them, click the gray arrows again to see the exact problem and then the exact location of the text error. Overset text means that text is spilling over the edge of a text frame twice here.

PRINT-READY PDF EXPORT

1. **File>Export>Adobe PDF (Print)**

This opens the settings dialogue box for exporting to Adobe PDF.

2. **Select 'Adobe PDF Preset: [PDF/X-1a:2001]'**

This setup takes care of most of the settings for you. All RGB colors are changed to CMYK, including photos and all transparency is smoothed so that professional printers and RIPs won't have any problems with it.

3. **Marks and Bleeds** (see picture below)

Check the box next to "crop marks," and then type 3mm for the top, bottom, left, and right bleeds.

4. **Output>Destination: Document CMYK – Coated FOGRA39 (ISO 12647-2:2004)** (see picture below)

This is where you pick which color profile to use when you change from RGB to CMYK. We have found that the polished FOGRA39 shape gives the best CMYK color change after a lot of tests.

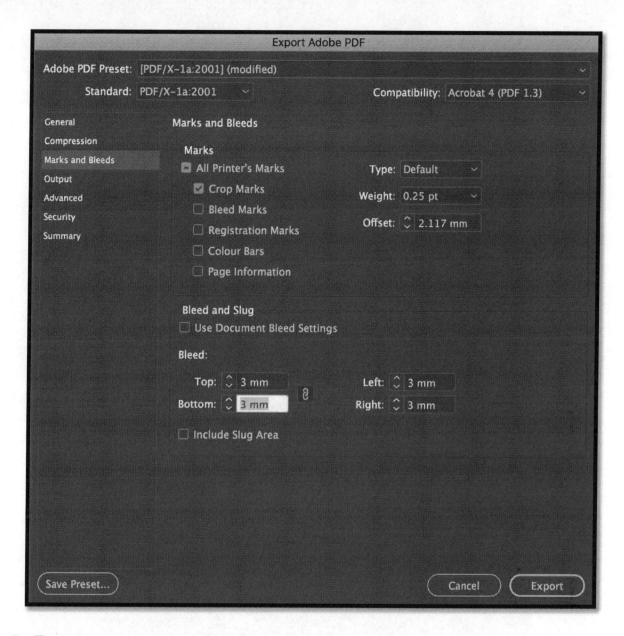

5. **Export**

Note: Don't click on "spreads." This makes spreads for readers, not spreads for printers. We need to cut reader spreads back into single pages so that we can put them in.

UNDERSTANDING PDF/X STANDARDS FOR PRINTING

There are PDF presets in InDesign that can help you make fewer choices and remember less. Many screens of options are organized by presets into the most common process groups, like business printing, desktop printing, and digital publishing. But can you really trust a setup to take care of the thing you spent so much time making? Also, how are you going to remember all of the different ways to print a PDF every time you need one? Do not worry about the learning curve; InDesign's PDF presets do not work on their own. If you've made PDFs with other Adobe Creative Cloud apps, you'll know some of the basic settings in InDesign. When using Illustrator or Photoshop to make PDFs, the presets are found in similar places. A flyout in the File menu makes it easy to get to InDesign's PDF settings. To see all of your choices, go to **File > Adobe PDF Presets**.

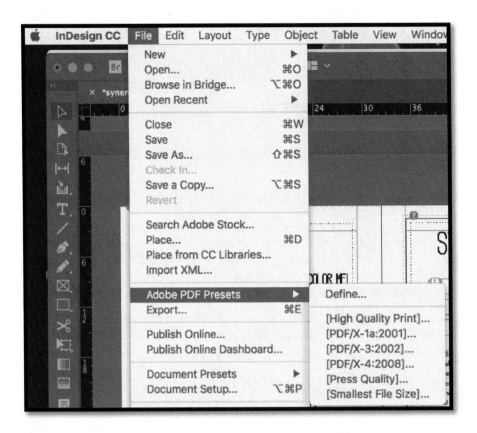

To quickly remember what a certain preset does, go to your InDesign project and choose **File > Adobe PDF Presets > Define**. As you choose a preset, you'll see a simple "Preset Description" right there in the dialog box.

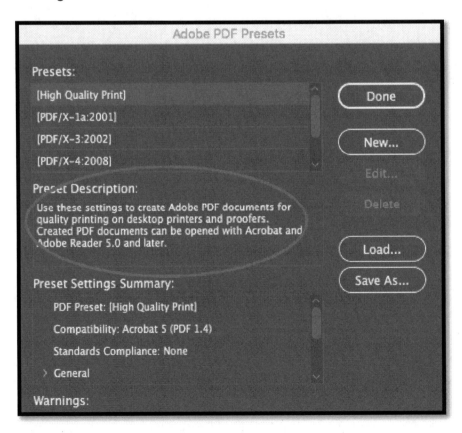

"High Quality Print" PDF Preset

For this setting, InDesign says that PDF files will be made that can be used for "high-quality printing on desktop printers and proofers." Which settings work best for this app? Photos in color or grayscale that have a quality of more than 300 ppi will be shrunk down to 300. Since the colors aren't changed, RGB and CMYK pictures will stay in the color spaces they were made in. Every setting for openness will also be left alone. Keep in mind that Acrobat and Acrobat Reader 5 are the bare minimum to work with these settings, which shouldn't be a problem these days.

What is PDF/X?

If your printer hasn't given you any instructions, PDF/X guidelines are the best thing to use. They're a good choice if you want to make sure your printer can open the file and cut down on printing issues. After talking to other makers and leaders in the industry, Adobe put together this set of ISO guidelines for print processes. Printers will often tell people to use the PDF/X presets because these standards are meant to make PDFs that can be printed by more people.

"PDF/X-1a:2001" PDF Preset

PDF/X-1a:2001 takes away the ability to work with Acrobat 5 and instead uses Acrobat 4. It doesn't matter if your colors are RGB or CMYK; they will all be changed to CMYK immediately. Any spot colors you've chosen will stay the same, though. You will also need to be careful about transparency flattening, and you might want to set the limits for your transparency treatment. Click "New" after selecting "PDF/X-1a:2001" under Define from the list of Adobe PDF Presets under "File."

Click "Advanced" on the left menu and then click "Transparency Flattener" on the right. Pick the "High-Resolution Transparency Flattener" setting if you want to keep the quality of your text and files. Photos with resolutions higher than 300 ppi will be lowered to 300 ppi.

PDF Preset "PDF/X-3:2002"

This setting will make your transparency flatten. Follow the same steps above if you want to choose your transparency settings ahead of time. PDF/X-3:2002 is like the old PDF/X choice in that embedded RGB profiles can be kept (they don't change automatically to CMYK). It's a useful setting if your printer wants to change the color settings based on where you're printing. This format is more popular with printers in Europe than in the United States.

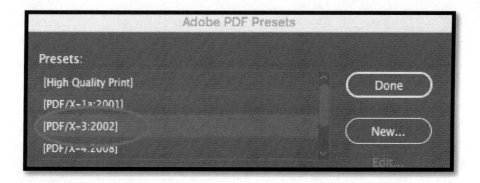

PDF Preset "PDF/X-4:2008"

You can keep any transparency in your document with this PDF/X present because the support is set to the most recent Acrobat 7. This is the most important thing that the PDF/X-4:2008 file does well. You can also keep any high-resolution photos in good shape. You can use colors like RGB, CMYK, and grayscale. You can still use LAB or ICC settings, and spot colors will not change.

PDF Preset "Press Quality"

This is another set of choices that are often used with professional printers that print at high quality. You can keep the document's transparency with this setting; you don't have to smooth it first. If you export a file in this way, Adobe Acrobat will be happy with it because it works well with live transparency and makes nice separations. Up to Adobe Acrobat 5 will be able to use it. If the real resolution is higher, all RGB values will be changed to CMYK, and the picture quality will be lowered to 300 ppi.

PDF Preset "Smallest File Size"

"Smallest File Size" is used most often on the web, where file size is important. This setting should be used for anything you want to share or show on a screen so that as many people as possible can see your document. Anything that has color and a high resolution will be instantly shrunk to 100 ppi. With up to 150 ppi, grayscale pictures can look very clear. You'll be able to work with files from as far back as Acrobat 6, and your layers and transparency will stay safe.

CUSTOM INDESIGN PRESETS

If you work in a business setting with a normal print process, the above choices will almost always get your documents ready to print. InDesign lets you change presets in a number of ways, in case you need to or just feel like getting fancy.

You don't have to talk about every possible standard change, but here are some ideas for everyday needs:

- To make your InDesign files dynamic after you've saved them as PDFs, go to File > Adobe PDF Presets > Define. Then, pick the setting you want to use and press "New."

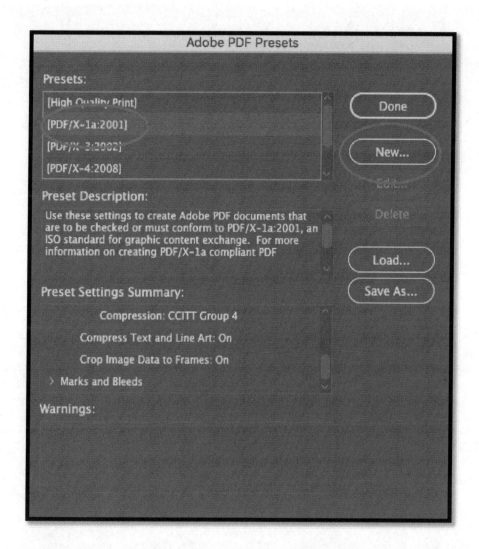

- **Choose "General" from the menu on the left, then choose the Hyperlinks and Interactive Elements you want from the list at the bottom of the screen:**

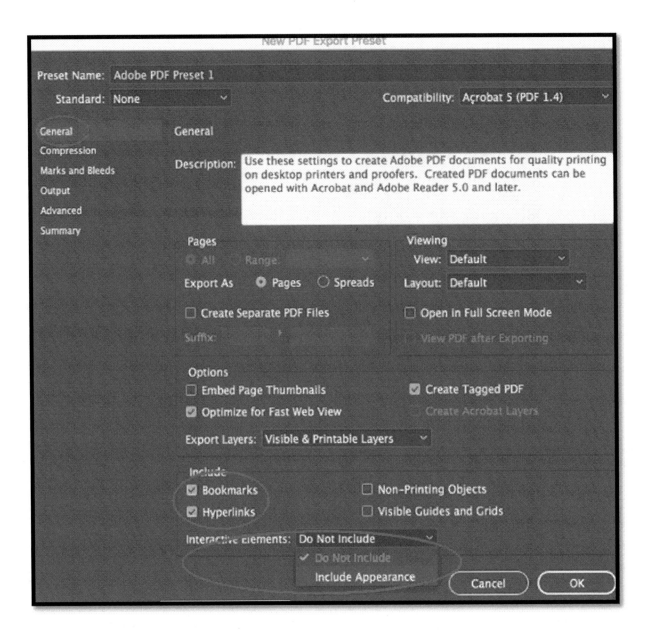

- To add crop marks, bleed marks, or other printer marks that your printer wants, go to **File > Adobe PDF Presets > Define**, pick your setting, and then press "New."

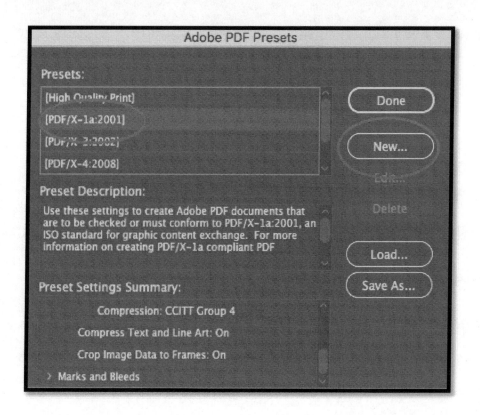

In the text box, choose "All Printer's Marks" in the upper screen and "Marks and Bleeds" from the choice on the left.

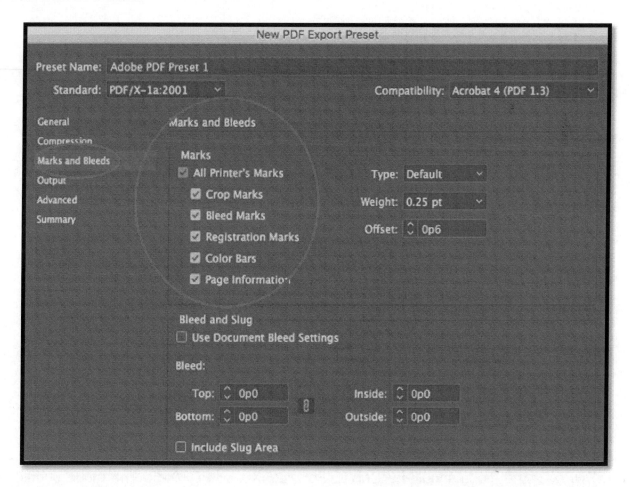

Saving your PDF Preset

Once you've made any more changes to any of InDesign's PDF Presets, give your preset a name in the box at the top of the screen. Click the "OK" button in the bottom right corner of the box.

Your setting will be put into the Adobe PDF Presets text box without you having to do anything.

PDF/X STANDARDS OVERVIEW

PDF/X-1a:2001 and PDF/X-3:2002

- **Intended Use**: The main reason for using it is for offset printing with CMYK color.

- **Color Spaces**: You can only use CMYK for color spaces.

- **Transparency**: Live transparency is not supported. All of the openness needs to be smoothed.

- **Fonts**: Fonts need to be built in.

- **Layers**: You can't use layers.

- **Image Compression**: You can't use JPEG 2000 to compress images.

PDF/X-4:2010 and PDF/X-5g: 2010

- **Intended Use**: The goal is to make it more adaptable and work with more color areas.

- **Color Spaces**: It works with spot colors, RGB, and CMYK.

- **Transparency**: You can be transparent in real-time.

- **Fonts**: Fonts need to be built in.

- **Layers**: You can use layers.

- **Image Compression**: You can compress images with JPEG 2000.

To make PDF/X-Compatible files, do these things:

- Get your InDesign file ready.

- Make sure that your document's color mode fits the PDF/X standard. For PDF/X-1a or PDF/X-3, the mode should be CMYK. For PDF/X-4 or PDF/X-5g, the mode should be RGB or CMYK.

- You can give your document the right color profiles by going to "Edit > Assign Profiles" in the menu bar.

- Make sure that every picture and color is in the right color area.

- Use the "Flattener Preview" panel for PDF/X-1a or PDF/X-3 to flatten transparency.

- Live transparency is allowed for PDF/X-4 or PDF/X-5g, but keep in mind that there may be problems when you print them.

- From the "File > Adobe PDF Presets" menu, choose the right PDF/X setting. Make sure that "Embed All Fonts" is checked in the export settings.

- Change the settings for picture compression based on the PDF/X standard you picked. PDF/X-4 and PDF/X-5g can work with JPEG 2000, but PDF/X-1a and PDF/X-3 can't.

- Figure out what kind of result you want for your paper. This is very important for making sure that colors look the same on all screens.

- Choose Adobe PDF (Print) from the "File > Export" menu. In the Export Adobe PDF window, choose the right PDF/X setting.

- Use the Preflight tool in Adobe Acrobat to look for problems and make sure the file meets the chosen PDF/X standard.

CHAPTER 13: AUTOMATING TASKS WITH SCRIPTS

INTRODUCTION TO SCRIPTS

People all over the world who work as workers use Adobe InDesign, which is desktop editing software. Scripts in InDesign are short pieces of code that are used to handle tasks that are done over and over again in the program. These scripts, which are written in JavaScript and can be run inside InDesign, can be used to handle a wide range of tasks and processes. Automation scripts can do tasks that would normally be hard to do and take a lot of time. This can greatly increase productivity and make processes easier.

One of the best things about using automation scripts in InDesign is that they can be used to handle tasks that are done over and over again. In this case, if you often make layouts with a certain style, color scheme, and font, you could make a script that will apply these settings to a new page immediately. This means you don't have to manually set up each piece, which saves you time and effort, keeps things consistent between projects, and lowers the chance of mistakes caused by people. To test, using automatic tools can also be very helpful in many ways. It is very important to make sure that everything is where it should be and working the way it should when you are working on long papers or complicated plans. Tests that look for problems or errors, like lost pictures, broken links, or wrong text layout, can be made with automation scripts. You can also look for types that are missing or make sure that engaging parts work. This way, creators can find issues and fix them before the project is finished. It is possible to simplify the testing process, which lets you find problems earlier and avoid costly mistakes at the same time. Automation scripts can do a lot more than just planning and testing. They can merge data, handle multiple files at once, and send files in different forms, among other things. For instance, if you need to make several copies of a document that are all translated into different languages, you can use an automatic script to put the translated text into the right layouts. This will make the whole process go more quickly and require fewer people to work on it.

BENEFITS AND APPLICATIONS OF AUTOMATION

Benefits

1. **Time Efficiency**:

   - **Batch Processing**: Doing things over and over again, like editing pictures, making sure that the entire layout is the same, or changing text in multiple documents, automatically can save a lot of time.

2. **Consistency**:

   - **Uniform Design**: Automation makes sure that styles, formatting, and design elements are used the same way throughout a document or across multiple documents, so the look and feel of all of them stay the same.

3. **Error Reduction**:

   - **Elimination of Manual Errors**: Automating normal jobs lowers the chance of mistakes made by people, which results in more accurate and error-free designs.

4. **Scalability**:

   - **Handling Large Projects**: Automation is especially helpful for taking on big, complicated projects because it streamlines processes and cuts down on the time needed for doing the same things over and over again.

5. **Improved Collaboration**:

   - **Standardization of Workflows**: Automation helps standardize workflows, which makes it easier for multiple team members to work together without any problems and follow the same steps.

6. **Quick Updates**:

   - **Dynamic Content Updates**: Automation makes it easy to quickly change things like prices, times, or contact information that change on multiple pages or documents.

7. **Resource Optimization**:

   - **Reduction in Workload**: Automation frees up designers' time by taking care of boring chores, so they can work on more creative and strategic parts of their jobs.

Page 114

Applications

1. **Data Merging**:

   - **Mail Merge**: If you want to make custom papers like letters or brochures by pulling information from a database, you can use data merging features.

2. **Templates and Master Pages**:

   - **Standardized Layouts**: Make templates and master pages to automatically plan parts that are used over and over again. This way, the structure of multiple pages or papers will be the same.

3. **Object Styles**:

   - **Consistent Formatting**: Object styles make it easy to apply uniform formatting to things like text frames, pictures, and shapes.

4. **Scripts**:

   - **Custom Automation**: You can write your own scripts or use existing ones to handle jobs that aren't covered by InDesign's built-in features. This makes InDesign more useful.

5. **Table of Contents and Indexing**:

   - **Automated Indexing**: Make live tables of contents and indexes based on the content of a document; these will update themselves automatically as the content changes.

6. **Preflighting**:

   - **Error Checking**: Set up preflight settings to check documents for problems automatically before they are printed or exported. This makes sure that the files are ready to print.

7. **Interactive Documents**:

   - **Buttons and Hyperlinks**: For digital or interactive documents, make it easy to add interactive elements like buttons, hyperlinks, and navigating tools by automating the process.

8. **PDF Export setups**:

   - **Streamlined Export**: Make export setups to automatically export documents to different forms with set parameters, making sure that the result is always the same.

WRITING AND EXECUTING CUSTOM SCRIPTS

Accessing the Script Editor

- To get to the Script Editor, start Adobe InDesign on your machine. In your browser, go to **Window > Utilities > Scripts** to get to the Scripts panel.

- In the Scripts panel, you can make new scripts, run existing scripts, and stack them in files if you want to.

- Right-click on the folder in the Scripts panel where you want to make a new script. This will begin the process of making the script. Click on "New Script" and then give it a name.

- Double-click on the script to open it in the script editor.

- This is where you write your JavaScript code.

- Save your script. Pick the story from the Scripts row. At the bottom of the screen, press the Run Script button which looks like a triangle.

- Use console.log () to print information for analysis. Know that the script editor can find issues with grammar.

Executing Custom Scripts

- To run custom scripts, go to **Window > Utilities > Scripts** and open the Scripts panel. Go to your script and double-click it to run it.

- Make a new InDesign file or open an old one. Under Edit, click on Keyboard Shortcuts.

- Pick Scripts from the Product Area menu. Make a link for your script.

- When you go to **File > Automate > Batch**, you can run a script on many files at once.

- Scripts may start running when you do certain things, like open or save a document. You can use the app.eventListeners.add() function to link scripts to events.

INTEGRATING SCRIPTS INTO THE WORKFLOW FOR EFFICIENCY

Adding scripts to your Adobe InDesign process may make it much more efficient by handling tasks that you do over and over, improving workflow, and making you more productive overall. The programming languages that Adobe InDesign can read are JavaScript, AppleScript (for macOS), and VBScript (for Windows). Adobe InDesign scripts are written in the computer language JavaScript. Some of the things that scripts can do automatically are making and handling items, saving papers, and editing text.

Accessing Scripts Panel

- To get to the Scripts Panel, open Adobe InDesign and choose the "Window" option. Go to **Utilities** and pick **Scripts**.

- Adobe InDesign mostly works with JavaScript as a programming language. For macOS users, AppleScript is another option, and for Windows users, VBScript is an option.

- Go to Adobe's website and read through the coding instructions for Adobe InDesign. To learn more about programming objects, properties, and methods, read this material.

- Open a script editor. For JavaScript, use the ExtendScript Toolkit. You can type or copy and paste your script code into the window. When you save the script, use the .jsx ending.

- In the Scripts panel, find the place where your script is saved. Double-click on the script to run it. Scripts can also be linked to special keys or buttons to make them easier to get to.

CHAPTER 14: IMPROVING EFFICIENCY WITH SHORTCUTS

KEYBOARD SHORTCUTS

Tools SHORTCUTS	🍎	⊞
Selection tool	V, Esc	V, Esc
Direct Selection tool	A	A
Toggle Selection and Direct	Cmd+Tab	Ctrl+Tab
Page tool	Shift+P	Shift+P
Gap tool	U	U
Pen tool	P	P
Add Anchor Point tool	=	=
Delete Anchor Point tool	-	-
Convert Direction Point tool	Shift+C	Shift+C
Type tool	T	T
Type On A Path tool	Shift+T	Shift+T
Pencil tool (Note tool)	N	N
Line tool	\	\
Rectangle Frame tool	F	F
Rectangle tool	M	M
Ellipse tool	L	L
Rotate tool	R	R
Scale tool	S	S
Shear tool	O	O
Free Transform tool	E	E
Eyedropper tool	I	I
Measure tool	K	K
Gradient tool	G	G
Scissors tool	C	C
Hand tool	H	H
Temporarily selects Hand tool	Spacebar (Layout mode), Opt (Text mode), or Opt+Spacebar (both)	Spacebar (Layout mode), Alt (Text mode), or Alt+Spacebar (both)
Zoom tool	Z	Z
Temp selects Zoom Intool	Cmd+Spacebar	Ctrl+Spacebar
Toggle Fill and Stroke	X	X
Swap Fill and Stroke	Shift+X	Shift+X
Toggle between Formatting Affects Container & Formatting Affects Text	J	J
Apply Color	, [comma]	, [comma]
Apply Gradient	. [period]	. [period]
Apply No Color	/	/
Switch between Normal View and Preview Mode	W	W
Frame Grid tool (horizontal)	Y	Y
Frame Grid tool (vertical)	Q	Q
Gradient Feather tool	Shift+G	Shift+G

Layers Panel SHORTCUTS		
Select all objects on layer	Option-click layer	Alt-click layer
Copy selection to new layer	Opt-drag small square to new layer	Alt-drag small square to new layer
Add new layer below selected layer	Command-click Create New Layer	Ctrl-click Create New Layer
Add new layer to the top of the layer list	Shift+Command-click Create New Layer	Shift+Ctrl-click Create New Layer
Add new layer to the top of the layer list and open New Layer dialog box	Cmd+Option+Shift-click Create New Layer	Shift+Alt+Ctrl-click Create New Layer
Add new layer and open New Layer dialog box	Option-click Create New Layer	Alt-click Create New Layer

Pages Panel SHORTCUTS		
Apply master to selected page	Opt-click master	Alt-click master
Base another master page on selected master	Opt-click the master you want to base the selected master on	Alt-click the master you want to base the selected master on
Create master page	Cmd-click Create New Page button	Ctrl-click Create New Page button
Display Insert Pages dialog box	Opt-click New Page button	Alt-click New Page button
Add new page after last page	Shift+Cmd+P	Shift+Ctrl+P

Character and Paragraph Styles SHORTCUTS		
Make character style definition match text	Select text and press Shift+Opt+Cmd+C	Select text and press Shift+Alt+Ctrl+C
Make paragraph style definition match text	Select text and press Shift+Opt+Cmd+R	Select text and press Shift+Alt+Ctrl+R
Change options without applying style	Shift+Opt+Cmd-double-click style	Shift+Alt+Ctrl-double-click style
Remove style and local formatting	Opt-click paragraph style name	Alt-click paragraph style name
Clear overrides from para-style	Opt+Shift-click parag style name	Alt+Shift-click paragraph style name
Show/hide Paragraph and Character Styles panels	Cmd+F11,Cmd+Shift+F11	F11, Shift+F11

Keys for the Control Panel SHORTCUTS	🍎	⊞
Toggle focus to/from Control panel	Cmd+6	Ctrl+6
Toggle Character/Paragraph text attributes mode	Cmd+Opt+7	Ctrl+Alt+7
Change reference point when proxy has focus	Any key (numeric)	Any key (numeric)
Display the pop-up menu that has focus		Alt+Down Arrow
Open Units & Increments Preferences	Opt-click Kerning icon	Alt-click Kerning icon
Open the Text Frame Options dialog box	Opt-click Number of Cols icon	Alt-click Number Of Cols icon
Open the Move dialog box	Opt-click X or Y icon	Alt-click X or Y icon
Open the Rotate dialog box	Opt-click Angle icon	Alt-click Angle icon
Open the Scale dialog box	Opt-click X or Y Scale icon	Alt-click X or Y Scale icon
Open the Shear dialog box	Opt-click Shear icon	Alt-click Shear icon
Open Text Preferences	Opt-click Superscript, Subscript, or Small Caps button	Alt-click Superscript, Subscript, or Small Caps button
Open the Underline Options dialog box	Opt-click Underline button	Alt-click Underline button
Open the Strikethrough Options dialog box	Opt-click Strikethrough button	Alt-click Strikethrough button
Open the Grids Preferences	Opt-click Align To Baseline Grid, or Do Not Align To Baseline Grid button	Alt-click Align To Baseline Grid, or Do Not Align To Baseline Grid button
Open the Drop Caps & Nested Styles dialog box	Opt-click Drop Cap Number Of Lines, or Drop Cap One Or More Characters icon	Alt-click Drop Cap Number Of Lines, or Drop Cap One Or More Characters icon
Open the Justification dialog box	Opt-click Leading icon	Alt-click Leading icon
Open Named Grid dialog box	Double-click Named Grid icon	Double-click Named Grid icon
Open New Named Grid Options dialog box	Opt-click Named Grid icon	Alt-click Named Grid icon
Open Frame Grid Options dialog box	Opt-click Number of characters Horizontal, Number of Characters Vertical, Character Aki, Line Aki, Vertical Scale, Horizontal Scale, Grid View, Font Size, Number of Columns, or Column Gutter icon.	Alt-click Number of characters Horizontal, Number of Characters Vertical, Character Aki, Line Aki, Vertical Scale, Horizontal Scale, Grid View, Font Size, Number of Columns, or Column Gutter icon

Keys for Panels SHORTCUTS	🍎	⊞
Delete without confirmation	Option-click Delete icon	Alt-click Delete icon
Create item and set options	Option-click New button	Alt-click New button
Apply value and keep focus on option	Shift+Enter	Shift+Enter
Activate last-used option in last-used panel	Command+Option+~ [tilde]	Ctrl+Alt+~ [tilde]
Select range of styles, layers, links, swatches, or library objects in a panel	Shift-click	Shift-click
Select nonadjacent styles, layers, links, swatches, or library objects in a panel	Command-click	Ctrl-click
Apply value and select next value	Tab	Tab
Move focus to selected object, text, or window	Esc	Esc
Show/Hide all panels, Toolbox, and Control panel (with no insertion point)	Tab	Tab
Show/Hide all panels except the Toolbox and Control panel (docked or not)	Shift+Tab	Shift+Tab
Open or close all stashed panels	Command+Option+Tab	Ctrl+Alt+Tab
Stash a panel group	Opt+drag any panel tab (in the group) to edge of window	Alt+drag any panel tab (in the group) to edge of screen
Select item by name	Opt+Cmd-click in list and then use keyboard to select item by name	Alt+Ctrl-click in list, and then use keyboard to select item by name
Open the Drop Shadow panel	Cmd+Opt+M	Alt+Ctrl+M

CREATING AND CUSTOMIZING SHORTCUT SETS

Change the active shortcut set

1. Make sure there are no other papers open if you want the trick to work for all of them.

2. Click Edit and then Keyboard Shortcuts.

3. From the Set menu, choose a button set. To give you an example, choose Shortcuts for QuarkXPress® 4.0.

4. Click the OK button.

View shortcuts

1. Click Edit and then Keyboard Shortcuts.

2. Pick a quick set for Set.

3. Choose the place with the directions you want to see in the Product place.

4. Pick an order from the list of commands. In the Current link area, the link is shown.

Generate a list of shortcuts for printing

1. Click Edit and then Keyboard Shortcuts.

2. Pick a quick set for Set.

3. Click on Show Set.

All of the present and unclear options for that set are shown in a text file when it starts.

Create a new shortcut set

1. Click Edit and then Keyboard Shortcuts.

2. Press "New Set."

3. Give the new set a name and choose an alternative set from the Based On Set menu. Then click OK to finish.

Create or redefine a shortcut

1. Click Edit and then Keyboard Shortcuts.

2. Click on Set and pick a shortcut set, or click on New Set to make a new one.

Note: You can't change the button sets for Default or QuarkXPress. Make a new set based on one of these sets instead, and then change the new set.

3. In the Product Area, choose the area that has the order you want to create or change.

4. Choose the command you want to create or change from the list of commands.

5. In the box that says "New Shortcut," press the keys that you want to use again and again. InDesign shows the other command under Current Shortcuts if the key sequence is already being used for another command. You could also change the first option, or you could try a different one.

Note: You shouldn't give menu options single-key shortcuts because they get in the way of typing text. If there is an entry point visible when you type a single-key shortcut, InDesign will use the shortcut instead of adding the character to the text.

6. In the list of contexts, choose the one where you want the computer action to work. The

context makes sure that the tool does what you want it to do. You can use Ctrl+G to join table cells (Table context) and Ctrl+G to add special characters (Text context), for example.

Note: You should assign tools in the Default context if you want them to work no matter what the document is doing at the moment. When you set shortcuts in a different context, like Table or Text, they take precedence over the shortcuts set in the Default context.

7. Pick one of these options:

   • Click "Assign" to make a new path where there isn't one already.

   • If you want to add another option to an action, click "Assign." There may be more than one computer option for a menu action.

8. Click OK to close the box, or click Save to keep it open while you add more links.

HIDDEN FEATURES AND PRODUCTIVITY HACKS

1. Create a Style Sheet for your styles

The most useful thing about InDesign is its paragraph style. Adding this option can make you much more productive and cut down on the time you spend organizing your files. Even though many people who use InDesign know how useful paragraph styles are and how they can help them make better layouts and save a lot of time, they still don't use them. Why does that happen? It can be hard to keep track of all the styles in a document, and sometimes it may not seem to make much sense. But styles are very important if you want to keep your look uniform, make changes that work well, or use tools like Hyperlinks or Table of Contents. Over the years, I designed my styles in a way that worked well for me, and I noticed that I used the same format in all of my papers. Even though I used the same approach every time, it took me about 3 to 4 hours to organize my styles for a typical job. That wasn't worth the time because I kept making the same layout over and over again. The font families used for the titles and the body were the little things that were always changing. Other small things that changed were things like spaces before paragraphs and so on.

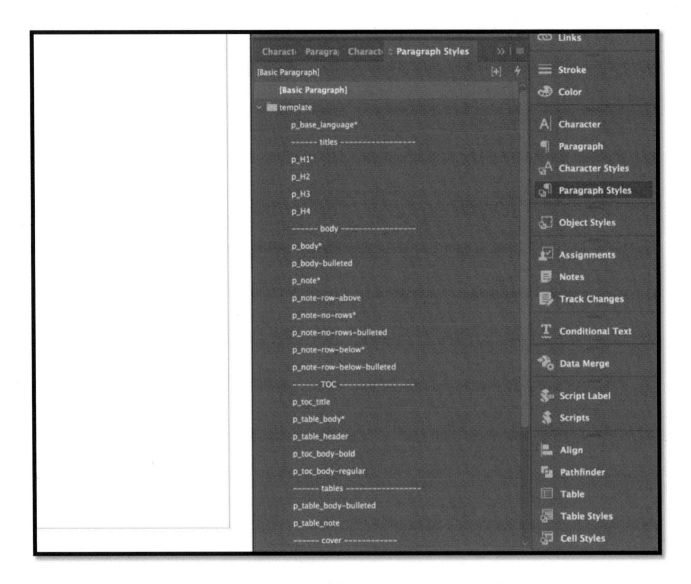

You can start a project right from the Style Sheet, or you can use it as a guide to make an InDesign file and then import the styles from that file. This first InDesign tip cut my start-up time from three to four hours to an hour or even less. You'll also make sure that all of your styles are set up correctly and that no setting is missing (for example, language, hyphenation), and by setting up "based on" and "next style" in your paragraph styles, you'll be able to speed up the whole process of making the document.

2. Use InDesign templates

People who work on a lot of papers with the same style or even content, like a user guide, a magazine, a newspaper, etc., might want to turn the Style Sheet idea we saw above into templates and add master pages, borders, grid lines, common parts, and so on. An InDesign template is a file that opens as a new, blank page when it is opened.

One clear benefit of starting a project from a template is that it saves time. It's also great when working with others because it makes sure that everyone starts from the same place. When working as a team, having files with the same structure also helps everyone work faster on the document. Naturally, you don't have to just work on your papers. You can also get an InDesign design (the link has the best one I could find online) and start working from that.

QUICKLY LAY OUT THE INFORMATION

Once you have a solid base for your project, the next step is to quickly add the information to your paper. Even though paragraph styles are very important, there are other tools that can assist you whether you are writing in InDesign for a book, a user guide, a catalog, or just for fun.

3. Use the primary text option

The text usually comes from a Word or RTF file that has already been organized. This is especially true for books and user guides. Then it's up to you to add this text to your paper and style it correctly. You know how long it takes to make all the pages and make sure the text flows right in the paper if you've done it before. This is something that InDesign can do for you. You can import the text with just a few clicks, and InDesign will make the pages and linked text frames for you. Just like magic!

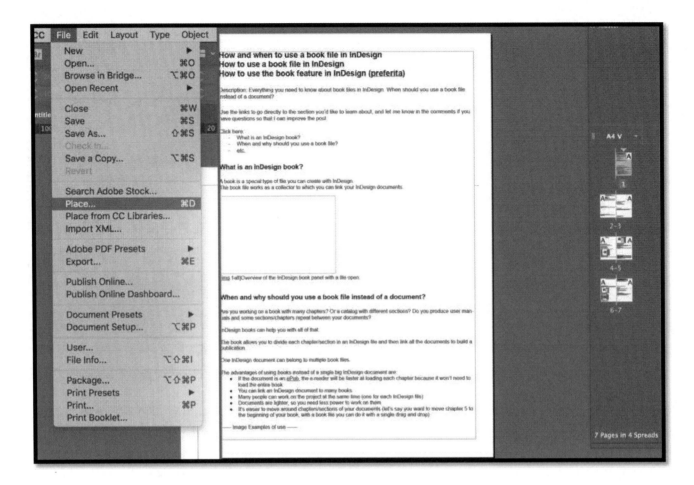

To do this, you need to set up your master pages, add a text frame to each master page, thread the text, and turn on the **"Primary Text Frame"** function. After that, you can bring the text into InDesign. This process can save you a lot of time and make the process of loading your text almost entirely automatic.

4. Data merge

Data join is a great way to save time, but a lot of people who use InDesign don't know about it. From a worksheet and a template, data merge lets you quickly arrange hundreds of pages with a **"repetitive layout."** These pages could be business cards, awards, or even catalogs. It speeds up the process, makes sure the plan is uniform, keeps me from making mistakes, and lets me give some jobs to my client. I use it every time I make a catalog.

When you make a list again, think about how it will be laid out and where you will put each piece of information. Split the file into several parts if you need more examples. Please have your client or coworker fill out an Excel file with the information you need. Then, make sure the file is ready to be used in the data merge process.

5. Use "Next Style"

We've seen how to add text or data to an InDesign project. But what if you pasted some text and want to quickly set the styles? This is another time when Paragraph Styles save the day and make things go more quickly and easily. We've seen that adding paragraph styles to your text can make it look great and uniform. You can give many chosen lines different styles with the **"Next Style"** feature. When you type in InDesign, "Next Style" also works. "Return" will tell InDesign to use the "Next Style" you chose for the new paragraph.

6. Learn how to use Anchored Object

When you anchor items in InDesign, you can make amazing automation. For instance, you could make a sign whose width changes immediately when the text does.

7. Use book files

It's also true that very few people use eBook files. If you want to keep all of your InDesign files together, you can use a book as a collection.

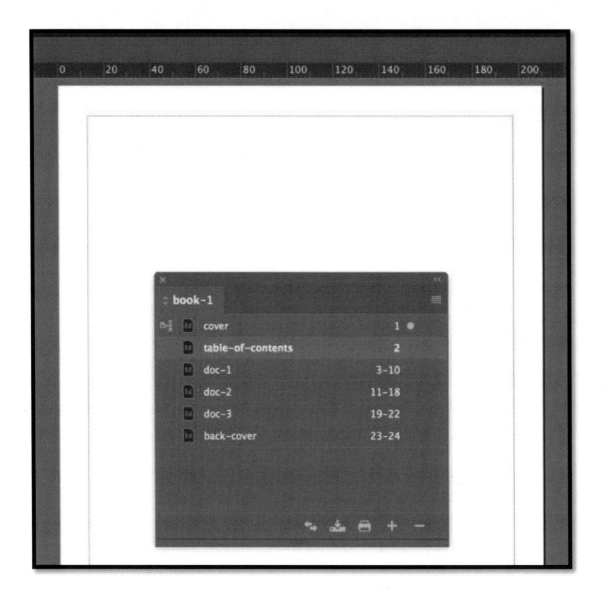

Book files let you divide a publication into smaller pieces that are easier to work on. This also lets other people at work on the same document, since it's split up into different files.

8. Use PDF presets

A PDF setup is a set of options that change how a PDF is made. Some settings in InDesign work for some designers, but not all of them make sense. It might be helpful to make your setup if you need to change the PDF export setting a lot, like when you want to add Marks or Bleeds. You can easily make your setting from the PDF export box. Make changes to the settings, then click "Save Preset." This simple tip might not save hours the first time you use it, but it will save you time every time. You will also make sure you don't forget to change any settings.

CHAPTER 15: SOLVING COMMON INDESIGN PROBLEMS

TROUBLESHOOTING DOCUMENT ERRORS

Color Management Challenges

Identifying Issues:

1. There are color differences throughout the whole paper (Paper 1).

2. Spot colors or changing between RGB and CMYK color modes don't work right.

How to Fix:

1. Use the "Preflight" screen to find and fix color problems, making sure that the document has a pleasant and consistent color scheme.

2. Make sure that all of the document's parts use the same color profiles. Differences in color profiles could confuse or distract readers.

3. If the paper is going to be printed, change the RGB pictures to CMYK. This step makes sure that the file will work with the printing process and that the colors will stay true.

TEXT OVERFLOW CHALLENGES

Identifying Issues:

1. The text goes beyond the edges of the text box that was set up.

How to Fix:

1. To quickly find cases of overflow, use the "Overset Text" sign in the bottom-right area of text frames.

2. Change the size of text frames or the text inside them to make sure it fits correctly in the frame.

Image Quality Concerns

Identifying Issues:

1. Some of the links in the "Links" part are missing or broken, which could make the page harder to view and use.

2. The pixelation in some pictures is caused by low quality, which makes the pictures look bad and less clear overall.

How to Fix:

1. Make sure the "Links" area works by checking for and fixing any broken or missing links

to make the user experience smooth.

2. Use the "Links" area to check the quality of a picture and make it better. To keep your presentation looking professional and nice to look at, replace pictures with smaller quality.

3. Think about how adding pictures or giving a high-resolution version when saving to PDF will affect people who are viewing from outside the document. This technique makes the paper look better and easier to read generally.

Additional Considerations:

- Check and update links often to keep information up-to-date and trustworthy.

- Use software for changing pictures to make the quality better, which will make them look more finished and professional.

- Work with the people who are making the material to make sure that the pictures meet high standards. This will help make the show look good and flow well.

Layering Challenges

Identifying Issues:

1. The visible ordering is broken because the layers are in the wrong order.

How to Fix:

1. Look over the layers panel to find and fix any problems with the order of the levels so that the visual structure is smooth.

2. Put layers in the right order to improve the design's general structure and flow.

3. Use the "Layers" tab to control which items can be seen, and make sure that parts are on the right levels and in the right order.

Additional Considerations:

- Check the layer structure often to make sure it can adapt to changes and improvements in the design.

- Use the layers panel's grouping and naming rules to make your work and teamwork go more smoothly.

- Work with your team to make sure that everyone is using the same layering style, especially on projects with a lot of workers.

RECOVERING FROM CRASHES AND UNEXPECTED ISSUES

It can be annoying when Adobe InDesign crashes or acts up for no reason, but there are things you can do to get your work back and figure out what's wrong. Here is a guide to help you get back to normal after Adobe InDesign crashes or does something strange:

1. **Turn on Auto-Recovery:**

   - In Windows, go to Edit > Preferences > File Handling; in Mac, go to InDesign > Preferences > File Handling.

   - Check the box next to "Automatically Save Recovery Data Every" and choose how often to save the data. This makes sure that InDesign backs up itself automatically.

2. **Check the Auto-Recovery Folder:** If InDesign crashes, it may have saved a recovery file. Find a file with the name ".indd" in the Auto-Recovery folder (the Preferences tell you where to find it).

3. **Save Incrementally:** Save your work regularly using incremental file names, like Project_v1.indd and Project_v2.indd. This makes several copies of the file in case it crashes, and you can go back to the most recent copy.

4. **Use file recovery services:** Adobe InDesign has a tool that lets you get back papers that you haven't saved yet. Click File, then Open Recent, and then click Recover Unsaved Documents. This could help you get back to recent changes.

5. **Turn off third-party plugins:** Crashes can be caused by third-party plugins that don't work with the main program or are broken. Turn off plugins for now to see if the problem still exists. In Windows, go to Edit > Preferences > Plugins. On a Mac, go to InDesign > Preferences > Plugins.

6. **Update InDesign:** Make sure you have the most recent version of Adobe InDesign. Updates often fix bugs and make improvements that can fix problems with stability.

7. **Check System Requirements:** Make sure your computer meets the system requirements for the version of InDesign you are using. The system requirements can be found here. Crashes can happen when the system doesn't have enough resources.

8. **Clear InDesign Cache:** Cache files that are damaged can cause problems you didn't expect. To clear the InDesign cache, start InDesign and hold down Ctrl + Alt + Shift (Windows) or Cmd + Opt + Shift (Mac).

9. **Create a New Document:** Open a brand-new, empty document and try pasting parts of the crashed document into it. This can help you narrow down the problem to a certain page or feature.

10. **Contact Adobe Support:** If the situation keeps happening, get in touch with Adobe Support. They can help you and may know about problems and answers that only happen with your version of InDesign.

OPTIMIZING INDESIGN PERFORMANCE FOR LARGE DOCUMENTS

We wish things would always go as smoothly and quickly as we'd like, but they don't always. Following some testing steps and being sure that the issue is not with a specific file or an object inside that file, there are a few things you can try to make InDesign run faster. And you know that your computer can usually handle the heavy work you have going on, then one or three of these issues and settings in InDesign could be stopping your machine from working right.

Set InDesign's Display Performance to Typical

The amount of processing power used goes up when you look at pictures at a high quality because InDesign has to keep redrawing parts as you move around the page. If you go to InDesign/Edit > Preferences > Display Performance and set the preset to Typical, the pictures will be shown at a quality that is good for screens. For a very long time, this has been the usual way for InDesign to show pictures on the screen. On the other hand, it looks like the most current version always sets to High Quality. It is possible to change how the present text is displayed if you right-click or control-click on a page. Another way to change the setting for just one picture is to right-click or control-click on it. This is still possible even when the sensitivity is set to high by default.

Turn off Live Drawing

If you want to get things done faster, turn off Live Screen Drawing in InDesign or at least set it to Delayed in the Interface tab of your Preferences. If you choose the "delayed" choice, you can see what the change will look like as you do it. If you click on an object, like a picture, and then wait a very short time before moving or changing it, this will happen. If you choose this choice right away, InDesign will have to show you each step of the process for each change. There is a lot of work to do.

Minimize Live Preflight

When you set the preferences for a certain result, Live Preflight works in the background to make sure that your document meets those preferences. It's probably working if you're not working. You can limit the pages that the Preflight panel looks at when you open it. The menu bar lets you do this by selecting Window > Output > Preflight. Alternatively, you can hit the Preflight option to the right of the red or green dot at the bottom of the document frame. Click on the radio button to the right of the "All" option at the bottom of the screen to choose a page or a different style. As of right now, the pre-flighting is only happening on that one page. Even better, you can turn it off totally by deselecting the "On" choice until the time you are ready to preflight.

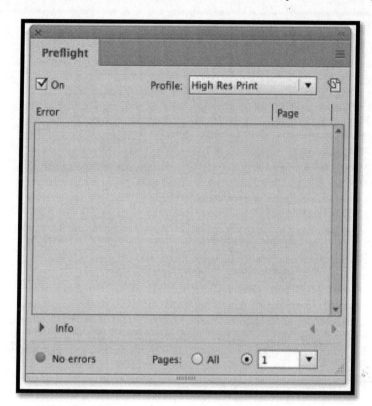

Turn Off Page Thumbnails

The pictures in your Pages box are working hard to keep up with you if your document has a lot of pages and each page has a lot of things on it. Even if they are redrawing, the images are not very useful because the page icons are often so small. For the most part, this is the case. To stop thumbnails from showing up on both pages and masters, go to the Pages panel menu and select Panel Options. Then, uncheck the box next to Show Thumbnails.

Turn Off Hyperlink Verification

There is a chance that a file with a lot of hyperlinks will load much more slowly because InDesign checks the URLs inside hyperlinks for validity all the time. If you want to stop checking the same URLs over and over, remove the "Auto Update URL Status" option from the Hyperlinks panel menu.

Disable the Save Preview Images feature

As you save your papers, InDesign gives you the choice to include a sample picture, which is also what it does by default. This is another thing that is always being changed while you are working. To make changes to this item, go to the Preferences menu and select the File Handling pane. By unchecking the "Always Save Preview Images" box, you can turn off the feature. At the very least, you could limit the sample pages to only the first one or two pages of the text. You could also limit the size of the preview itself.

CHAPTER 16: EXPLORING ADVANCED TYPOGRAPHY

OPENTYPE FEATURES

- First, pick a font that works with OpenType features. A lot of modern and professional fonts offer a lot of stylistic choices.

- The names of OpenType fonts often tell you what they can do, like "Pro," "Std," or "OpenType."

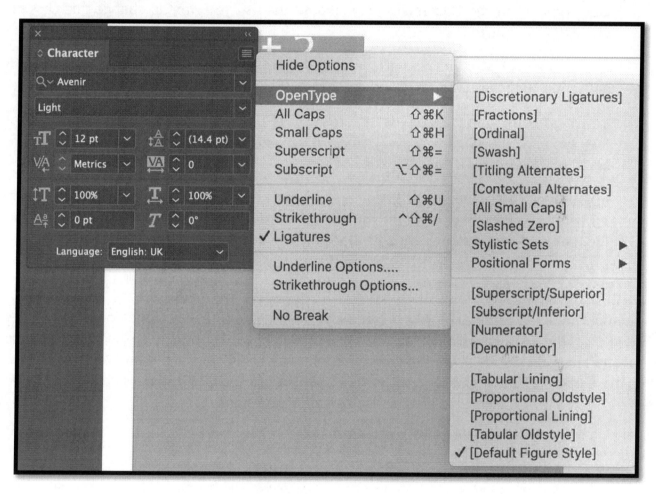

- You can get to the Glyphs panel in InDesign by going to Window > Type & Tables > Glyphs.

- This panel lets you see and type in single glyphs, including those with special characters and ligatures.

- Ligatures are groups of two or more characters that are meant to look better when they are used together. In the Character box, select the word and choose the "Ligatures" choice. This will make the ligatures appear.

- There are swashes and other symbols in some fonts that can be found in the Glyphs panel. Look for people who have beautiful flair.

- The Stylistic Sets choice in the Character panel lets you pick from some different sets of styling options for characters.

- "Contextual alternatives" are character types that are changed instantly based on the other characters around them. In the OpenType panel, contextual options can be turned on or off.

- A lot of the time, OpenType fonts have special characters for working with fractions. The Glyphs panel or the Fraction choice in the Character panel can be used to get to these.

- True small caps, which are meant to look and feel like capital letters, can be used with OpenType. From the Character menu, choose the text you want to change and click on the "tiny Caps" button.

- To get to special characters like ordinals (1st, 2nd, and 3rd) or superscripts and subscripts, use the Glyphs or Character windows.

- You might want to add OpenType features to the Paragraph and Character Styles so that they are used the same way every time. This makes sure that the styles are applied the same way everywhere on your page.

- If you want to see how your document will look with OpenType features added, use InDesign's Preview mode. When you export your file, like PDF, make sure you choose the "embed fonts" option so that the OpenType features stay in the final file.

IMPLEMENTING LIGATURES, SWASHES, AND ALTERNATE CHARACTERS

A normal ligature in fonts takes two or three characters and puts them together to make one. This kind of ligature helps with kerning when one character moves into the space left by the next character. In each tongue, there are different ligatures. This is because many words in English use the letters ff, ffi, fi, and fl together. When you use ligatures, be careful because they can stand out a lot if your text has a lot of space between the letters.

Another kind of ligature is an optional ligature, which is usually just for looks. Also, these ligatures join two or three characters together to make a single, beautiful design. There are combinations like TH, th, ck, ct, et, and st. There are also double characters like oo, tt, and ll. This kind of binding needs to be used carefully, just like any other kind. It's important to make it clear that not all fonts have standard and optional ligatures. Each font is unique, and it's up to the font creator to decide which ones to use.

HOW TO USE LIGATURES IN INDESIGN

Step 1

Make a new file in Adobe InDesign by opening it. To get to the Glyphs panel, go to Window > Type > Glyphs. To turn ligatures on or off, go to Window > Type > Character and open the Character box. To turn them on or off, click the button in the upper right spot and choose Ligatures.

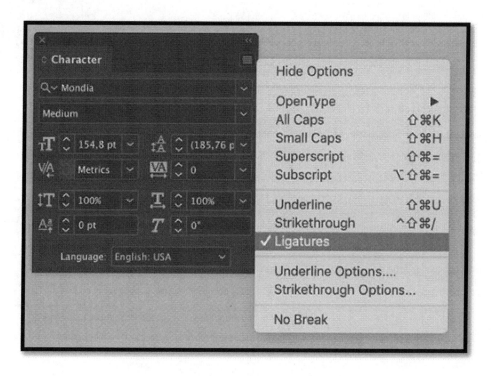

Step 2

Pick up the Text Tool (T) from the menu bar and type anything you want. I'll use "THE TWIN MOON INN" for this lesson. Change the font to Mondia.

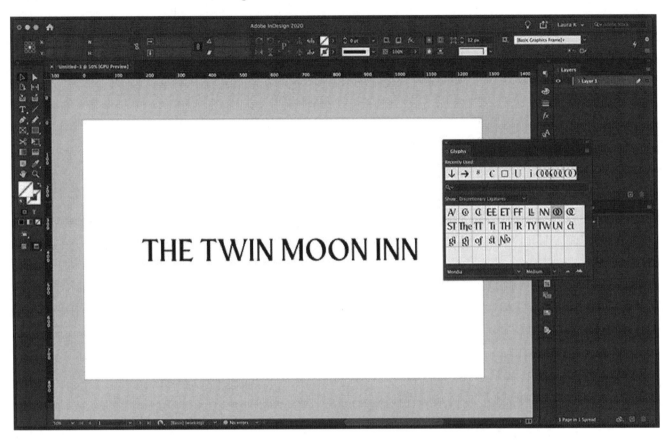

Step 3

Set the group of icons to Standard Ligatures in the icons panel. Use the **Text Tool (T)** to choose the pair of characters you want to change in the Glyphs box. Then, use the ligatures. In the Glyphs panel, double-click on the style you want to use. If you want the ligatures to show up immediately, make sure you turn them on in the Character box.

ACCESS ALTERNATE CHARACTERS IN INDESIGN?

Option #1 - Select a letter

For different people, this works.

1. Pick out the letter you want to change.

2. If there is a different image, a small box will appear.

3. Click on the different option you want to add.

Option #2 - Access via the glyphs panel

For different letters and ligatures, this works.

1. Go to the top menu and choose Type > Glyphs or Window > Type & Tables > Glyphs.

2. In the upper right corner, choose the type you want to use.

3. Select a letter or use the type tool to select a character, and then click on a character you want to add.

Establishing an effective typographic hierarchy

Setting up a good typography order in Adobe InDesign is important for making papers that look good and are easy to read. Typographic order organizes and ranks information to help the reader find their way through the text. To set up a strong stylistic order in Adobe InDesign, follow these tips:

1. **Heading Styles:**

   - Put different amounts of information under different heading styles (e.g., Heading 1, Heading 2, etc.).

   - Use the same font family, size, and color for all levels of headings.

   - Change the leading (line spacing) to make it easy to tell the difference between headers and body text.

2. **Font Choice:**

   - Use a few different fonts to keep the look professional and unified.

   - Pick styles that go well with each other. It is normal to use a serif font with a sans-serif script.

3. **Font Size:**

   - Use bigger font sizes for more important information and smaller ones for less important information.

- Lower-level text and body text should have font sizes that are gradually smaller.

4. **Font Weight:**

   - Use different font weights (like normal, bold, and light) to draw attention to and away from writing.

   - Make sure that the difference in weight is clear but not too much.

5. **Color:**

   - Smartly use color to draw attention to certain parts. As an example, you could use a bright color for the headings and a dull color for the text.

   - Make sure the difference in color between the text and the background is big enough to read.

6. **Spacing:**

   - Change the distance between lines (leading) and between letters (tracking) to make the text easier to read.

   - Make good use of white space (like borders and gaps) to make the plan look clean and well-organized.

7. **Alignment:**

   - Align the text in the same way all over the page. Based on how the text looks, you can choose between left, center, right, or justified orientation.

8. **Consistency:**

   - Use the same fonts and styles throughout the whole paper to make it look professional and put together.

   - Set a flow by using the same font types and sizes for parts that go together.

9. **Hierarchy with Scale:**

   - Use a scale of letter sizes to make a clear visual order. For instance, the main titles might be a lot bigger than the subheadings, and so on.

10. **Contrast:**

    - To draw attention to important information, use contrast by changing the font size, weight, and style.

    - Play around with different combos until you find one that looks good and works well.

11. **Preview and Adjust:**

- Look over your paper often to make sure the font structure is clear and uniform.

- Make changes as needed based on what people say and what you can see.

CHAPTER 17: EXTENDING INDESIGN WITH PLUGINS AND SCRIPTS

CREATE, INSTALL, AND MANAGE PLUGINS

The InDesign plugin modules are pieces of software made by Adobe and other companies that work with Adobe to add extra features. There are a lot of importing, exporting, scripting, and special effects plugins that come with your program and are set up immediately in the Plugins area. Plugins are what give you most of the tools you see in InDesign.

Install plugins

Plugin modules show up as choices on menus, dialogs, or windows after they are enabled.

Create InDesign plugins with UXP

It is now possible to use current JavaScript (ES5 and most of ES6) in InDesign plugins thanks to the Unified Extensibility Platform (UXP).

INTEGRATION WITH CREATIVE CLOUD ADD-ONS VIA THE BROWSE ADD-ONS MENU

Within the Adobe Exchange website, you can look for and set up add-ons, apps, and more for Adobe InDesign and other programs.

- To add the extra tools to InDesign, go to **Window > Browse Add-ons**. You can get these extras for free or for a fee. This process syncs all the tools you've downloaded or updated from the Creative Cloud app for InDesign with InDesign. It gets you to the page where you can view add-ons.

- You can then see these add-ons in **Window > Extensions, Downloads**, or the place stated in the add-on's description. Go to the explore add-ons page and look for "View my add-ons" in the menu on the left. This will show you the add-ons you've downloaded. It also shows which items and versions of those goods these add-ons work with.

If you turn on file sync, the search add-ons will connect to your Creative Cloud account.

INSTALLING AND MANAGING EXTENSIONS

You can add different features to InDesign by installing plugins. To do this, you must first go to Adobe's website. In this case, you need to use exchange.adobe.com. If you look for this Adobe page, it will show up. Go to the "Creative Cloud" tab on this page. On this page, scroll down and pick InDesign from the list of goods. It will show you all the tools that work with InDesign once you choose it. You could also open InDesign and go to the Windows menu. Choose "Find Extensions on Exchange" from the list that comes up.

If you pick that choice, InDesign will take you to the website for the Adobe InDesign app. It will ask you to log in if you are not already. Then, click the "Free" button to make it possible to install. It will ask you to agree to the terms and conditions, which you should do. There will also be a box that says "Install." Click that. If you have any issues, please visit the Installation help part of this page. You will be taken to this page when you choose the "help" choice. From this page, you can download the given application right away. If you click on Download, you will get an installation file. Then, follow the steps below to properly install the app you chose. Install the raw file with Adobe's Creative Cloud PC program once you have it in the format you want. Now it will take you to the page where you can download the extension manager. Here is where you can click to download.

After you've gotten it, put it in. When you put it in, it will look like this. In this window box, the Install tab is in the top left area. Click on it. When you click the Install button, a new box will show up where you can pick the installation file for the extension you chose. When the extension manager is done running, it will show a message that says "successfully installed." If the application you installed is not where you thought it would be in InDesign, go back to the page where you installed it. You'll see the words "Where to discover It'll" further down. You can read the writing by clicking on it, and this is where you can find this extension in your InDesign program. If you already have InDesign open, close it and then start it again to see these changes. Then, go to the Window menu. In its drop-down menu, we can choose "Extension." Your added app will show up in the sub-drop-down menu.

Removing an InDesign Extension

We no longer need a few of the tools they came with, so we need to remove them from our program for different reasons. Here's what you can do to make it happen. If you used the InDesign Creative Cloud app to add your extension, use the extension manager to open it. When you open one of them, a list of everything you've loaded will show up. Pick out what you want to get rid of. Once you've picked the one you want, click the "Remove" button in this box. It will only take a few seconds to remove the app you picked. The old extension might still be in the list of loaded extensions if you check it again in InDesign. This is because you have to restart the app to see the changes.

FREQUENTLY ASKED QUESTIONS

What is InDesign and who is it for?

Adobe InDesign is a complex program for workers who work with both paper and digital printing to lay out pages. The software comes with all the tools you need to create, test, and share a wide range of material for print, the web, and tablet apps, among other formats. Users of InDesign can fine-tune fonts, use creative tools that come with the program, and work in an easy-to-use design environment. The software works well with other Adobe products, like Photoshop, Illustrator, Acrobat, and Adobe Animate, making it easy for creative workers to get their work done. A wide range of people can use InDesign, such as artists, people who work in prepress and production, and print service providers. People who work in magazines, design firms, advertising agencies, newspapers, book publishers, retail/catalog companies, business design, commercial printing, and other advanced publishing settings are among its target audience. The app meets the specific needs of these workers by giving them a strong base for making papers that look good and are well organized. One big benefit of using InDesign is that it is part of the Adobe Creative Cloud environment. As soon as new changes and releases are ready, subscribers can get them. This makes sure that users always have access to the newest features and improvements. Users with a Creative Cloud All Apps plan can also use Adobe Digital Publishing Suite, Single Edition" with InDesign. This lets them create and package an endless number of single-edition iPad apps that can be uploaded to the Apple App Store.

How does InDesign integrate with other Adobe products?

It's not just a technology merger; Photoshop, Illustrator, Flash Professional, and InDesign all use the same user interface, instructions, panels, and tools. The shared framework makes learning easier for users because they can use what they know from one program when switching to another. Moving quickly between Adobe programs is easy thanks to the uniform design, which makes the experience smooth and natural. One of the best things about InDesign's inclusion is that you can easily load Photoshop and Illustrator files. Using this feature makes it easier to lay out, improve, and update images in the InDesign setting. Users can easily add files from these programs, which keep the design's purity and reduce the amount of work needed to handle visual elements. Another useful aspect of InDesign is that it can directly open PDF files. This makes sure that the output is reliable and uniform across all printing forms, such as print, web, and smartphones. This support makes it easier to share and keeps the look of papers the same no matter what output source is picked. InDesign and Flash Professional work well together, so users can easily move page layouts between the two programs while keeping any motion, sound, or video files that are contained in the documents. This makes sure that the quality stays good when switching between the two programs, giving you a smooth multimedia experience. Also, InDesign and InCopy work together to give small creative teams a powerful editing process management system. This teamwork makes it easier for artists and writers to work together and talk to each other. It also speeds up the editing process and makes content creation more efficient and team-based.

What is the InDesign family of products?

The main product of a combined publishing family is Adobe InDesign. It is joined by InCopy and InDesign Server. This connected environment is made to help with different parts of the publishing process by giving you specific tools for writing, rewriting, working together, and using server-based solutions. InCopy is a professional writing and editing tool that works well with InDesign and is an important part of this family. The main goal is to make it easier for artists, writers, and editors to work together on editing processes. By working together with InDesign, InCopy makes it easy for everyone involved in the content creation process to work together. The artistic Cloud All Apps plan gives users full access to Adobe's full suite of artistic tools, and InCopy is one of them. InDesign Server is the most advanced member of the family; it adds writing and layout features to a server platform. This new feature adds a higher level of automation to editing processes, making material, customizable printing based on data, and web-to-print solutions that use templates. InDesign Server is made to make things bigger and easier. It has advanced workflow features that make huge printing settings more efficient and productive. When used together, InDesign, InCopy, and InDesign Server make a strong environment that meets the many needs of printing pros. This unique publishing process makes it easier for everyone involved to work together.

Does InDesign provide a solution for large publishing environments?

Yes. Systems developers around the world can offer printing systems that work both with InDesign and InCopy if you need a custom solution built on core InDesign technology.

Should QuarkXPress users convert to InDesign?

Yes. InDesign has been used by publishers all over the world, from small design groups to large printing companies. InDesign is the best choice for printing settings that move quickly because it has a strong partner community, is backed by an industry leader, and is user-driven.

In what languages can InDesign files be created and shared?

You can open and change Indic, Japanese, Middle Eastern, Chinese, and Korean layouts in Roman and Indic versions of InDesign. You can also do the same with Japanese, Middle Eastern, Chinese, or Korean versions of Roman and Indic files. But the Roman versions of InDesign don't have the stylistic, layout grid, and frame grid tools that the Japanese, Middle Eastern, Chinese, and Korean versions do. These tools are needed to change text in the Middle East and Asia.

What is an InDesign Server?

With InDesign Server, you can manage the design, layout, and typography features of InDesign. It is a strong, highly flexible, and scalable layout and composition engine. It uses the same code base as InDesign and can run a lot of different automatic printing solutions, such as web-to-print, VDP, and editing workflow solutions. It also gives you the same high-quality output as InDesign. Most systems that use InDesign Server are based on models that designers made with the desktop version of InDesign.

How does InDesign differ from InDesign Server?

There are some important changes between InDesign Server and the PC version of InDesign, even though they share the same code base:

- InDesign Server is a tool that runs bigger automatic printing systems.

- InDesign Server is an empty program, which means it doesn't have a user interface built in. A customer or a solution partner would make a user interface that works with the automatic printing system that InDesign Server runs.

- You can use scripts or C++ plug-ins to control InDesign Server, just like you can with InDesign. It can be controlled by a SOAP interface or Java APIs, though. You can also use the Flex framework and Adobe Flash Builder (sold separately) to create interesting Rich Internet applications (RIAs) that run in web browsers or as stand-alone clients with the Adobe AIR runtime. The scalable and reliable back-end server is the InDesign Server.

- Automated printing systems that use InDesign Server can grow as needed because they can run multiple versions on different computers.

- InDesign Server has been tried thoroughly to help make sure it works well for long amounts of time.

- InDesign Server was made to work on server versions of Windows and Mac OS, including Microsoft Windows Server 2008 R2.

- You can't get an InDesign Server with Creative Cloud; you have to buy it separately.

CONCLUSION

As we come to the end of "Mastering Adobe InDesign 2024: A Guide for Beginners," it is important to reflect on the journey we've undertaken through this comprehensive guide. Adobe InDesign is an incredibly powerful and versatile tool that, when mastered, opens up a world of possibilities for creating professional-quality designs and publications. This book has been designed to provide a thorough understanding of InDesign 2024, equipping you with the skills and knowledge needed to harness its full potential.

Reflecting on the Learning Journey

Starting from the basics, we explored the fundamental aspects of Adobe InDesign, laying a solid foundation for more advanced topics. Understanding the key feature updates in InDesign 2024 was crucial, as these enhancements significantly improve both the user experience and the overall design process. Features like Auto Style, Hide Spreads, and the improved Publish Online function are designed to streamline workflows and offer new creative possibilities.

As we delved into setting up your workspace, it became evident how customization and efficiency are paramount in creating an optimal working environment. By configuring the workspace to suit individual preferences and needs, users can work more effectively and with greater comfort. The ability to create custom workspaces, manage panels, and utilize the application bar and tools panel efficiently plays a crucial role in boosting productivity.

Document Creation and Management

The process of document creation, from using templates and presets to modifying and creating new documents, forms the core of many InDesign projects. This book guided you through these processes, ensuring you can start any project on the right foot. The importance of understanding the New Document dialog and utilizing parent pages cannot be overstated, as they provide the structure and consistency needed for professional publications.

Managing documents efficiently also involves mastering the art of text and typography. InDesign 2024's robust text tools and advanced typographic settings allow for precise control over text layout and formatting. By learning to create and manage text frames, apply paragraph and character styles, and utilize nested styles, you can ensure that your documents are both visually appealing and easy to read.

Advanced Design Techniques

Our exploration of advanced design techniques, including text wrapping, anchored objects, and table creation, highlighted the versatility of InDesign 2024. These features enable designers to handle complex layouts with ease, integrating text and graphics seamlessly. The ability to wrap text around images, create and format tables, and manage lengthy documents with book features are essential skills for any advanced InDesign user.

Working with images and graphics is another critical aspect of InDesign, and this book provided detailed insights into inserting, resizing, and formatting visual elements. The Place command, frame fitting options, and links panel are indispensable tools for managing images effectively. Additionally, understanding how to work with vector graphics and the integration of Adobe Creative Cloud apps further expands your design capabilities.

Color Management and Interactive Elements

Effective color management is crucial for ensuring that your designs look as intended across different mediums. InDesign 2024 offers a range of tools for applying and managing color, including swatches, spot colors, and color libraries. By mastering these tools, you can achieve consistent and accurate colors in your designs, whether for print or digital output.

Interactive documents represent an exciting frontier for InDesign users, and this book covered the creation of hyperlinks, cross-references, buttons, and forms. These interactive elements enhance user engagement and make digital publications more dynamic and functional. The improved Publish Online function and integration with Google Analytics provide valuable insights into how your interactive documents are being used, helping you refine and improve your content.

Collaboration and Version Control

Collaboration is a key aspect of modern design workflows, and InDesign 2024 offers robust tools for working with others. Integration with Adobe InCopy allows for seamless collaborative editing, enabling multiple users to work on the same document simultaneously. This collaboration is vital for large projects, ensuring that all team members can contribute effectively.

Version control features help you keep track of changes and manage different versions of your documents, ensuring that your team is always working with the most up-to-date content. These tools are essential for maintaining consistency and quality in collaborative projects, providing the structure and control needed to manage multiple contributors effectively.

Prepress, Printing, and Automation

Preparing your documents for print involves several critical steps, from preflighting and PDF export to understanding PDF/X standards. InDesign 2024 provides comprehensive tools to ensure that your documents are print-ready and meet industry standards. By following best practices for prepress and printing, you can avoid common pitfalls and ensure that your printed materials are of the highest quality.

Automation and scripting are powerful features that can significantly enhance your workflow. By automating repetitive tasks and creating custom scripts, you can save time and increase efficiency. This book covered the basics of scripting, providing the knowledge needed to start integrating automation into your design process.

Troubleshooting and Optimization

No design process is without its challenges, and InDesign 2024 includes features to help you troubleshoot common issues and optimize performance. From resolving text overflow and image quality concerns to managing layers and recovering from crashes, this guide provided practical solutions to keep your projects on track.

Optimizing InDesign's performance, especially for large documents, involves configuring settings and preferences to minimize resource usage and maximize efficiency. By following best practices for performance optimization, you can ensure that InDesign runs smoothly, even with complex and resource-intensive projects.

Advanced Typography and Customization

Typography is a fundamental aspect of design, and InDesign 2024 offers advanced tools for creating sophisticated typographic layouts. The integration of OpenType features, ligatures, swashes, and alternate characters allows for greater creative expression and precision. Understanding and utilizing these features can elevate the quality of your designs and set them apart from the competition.

Customization options, including the creation and management of plugins and extensions, provide additional ways to tailor InDesign to your specific needs. By leveraging these advanced features, you can push the boundaries of your design work and create truly unique and compelling layouts.

Moving Forward with Confidence

"Mastering Adobe InDesign 2024: A Guide for Beginners" has provided you with a comprehensive foundation in one of the most powerful design tools available today. As you continue to explore and use InDesign, remember that mastery comes with practice and experimentation. Don't be afraid to try new techniques, explore advanced features, and push the limits of what InDesign can do.

This book is not just a guide but a starting point for your journey with Adobe InDesign 2024. The skills and knowledge you have gained here will serve as a solid foundation for future growth and development. Whether you are creating print publications, digital content, or interactive documents, InDesign offers the tools and flexibility to bring your creative visions to life.

Embracing Continuous Learning

The world of design is constantly evolving, and staying up-to-date with the latest trends and technologies is essential for any designer. Adobe regularly updates InDesign with new features and improvements, so it's important to continue learning and exploring these updates to stay ahead of the curve.

Consider joining online communities, attending webinars, and participating in workshops to further enhance your skills. The Adobe Creative Cloud community is a valuable resource for learning from other designers, sharing ideas, and staying informed about the latest developments in design software and techniques.

Final Thoughts

Adobe InDesign 2024 is a powerful tool that offers immense possibilities for designers of all levels. This book has aimed to provide a thorough understanding of its features and capabilities, helping you to become a proficient and confident InDesign user. By mastering the skills and techniques covered in this guide, you can create professional-quality designs that stand out and make an impact.

Remember, the key to mastering InDesign, or any design tool, is practice and experimentation. Don't be afraid to push boundaries, try new things, and learn from your experiences. With dedication and creativity, you can unlock the full potential of Adobe InDesign 2024 and take your design work to new heights.

Thank you for joining us on this journey through Adobe InDesign 2024. We hope this guide has been informative and inspiring, and we wish you the best of luck in all your future design endeavors. Keep creating, keep learning, and most importantly, keep pushing the limits of what you can achieve with Adobe InDesign.

Made in the USA
Columbia, SC
12 November 2024

46327941R00124